Cassandra's Crossing

The Future of Public Schooling?

Russell L. Hamm

VANTAGE PRESS
New York / Los Angeles / Chicago

Published by Vantage Press, Inc.
516 West 34th Street, New York, New York 10001

Manufactured in the United States of America
ISBN: 0-533-08033-9

Library of Congress Catalog Card No.: 88-90166

To Levi Clark Bennett

Contents

Acknowledgments

A special thanks to Marianne Mazley-Allen, Sue Lightfoot, and Christy Watts for their help in the preparation of this manuscript.

The Title

Cassandra was a prophet, and because she did not return Apollo's love, he punished her by ordering no one to believe her prophecies—true though they were. She warned against holding Helen of Troy captive, and she warned against bringing the Wooden Horse within the walls of Troy. When Troy fell, she was taken captive by the Greeks. Later she was murdered.

Crossing refers to the fact that public schooling as a viable institution in our democratic society is at risk. The hope is that public schools will not again become "pauper" schools, but will become a vital and necessary ingredient to our democratic society.

Mediagate

The subject [is] not . . . remote, philosophical, or esoteric.
—Adolf A. Berle, Jr., *Power*

The most powerful force in American society today is that of the mass media.† And who is to hold this center of power accountable? "Ah, yes," they cry, "freedom of the press!"—if one has the audacity to criticize or question. They say, "We don't *make* the news; we only report it." But news is ubiquitous. Who chooses what is "fit to print" (broadcast)? (Note: They even choose the letters to the editor.) But a truly free press is a responsible press. How easy it is for this center of power to manipulate emotions, to propagandize ideas for its own ends.

The media are aggressive in their stance against censorship—overt, blatant. But the worst censors are the media—in benign neglect of major news events, in advocacy of certain political-social stances. The media profess objectivity, when objectivity is a myth.

In their arrogance in checking out other institutions as to morality, ethics, perhaps they protest too much. As Lord Acton said in 1887, "Power tends to corrupt and absolute power corrupts absolutely."

As Adolf A. Berle (1969) wrote: "Danger exists when any substantial body of opinion is not involved in dialogue. Any group having no means of expressing its views within an organized dialogue must either be quiescent or obstruct, demonstrate, or perhaps rebel" (p. 118).

---

* Originally published in *Contemporary Education* 49, no. 1 (Fall 1987), p. 5. Used by permission.
† The singular form is used intentionally.

Introduction

Public schooling is at a crossroads. The future may see public schools as simply warehouses for the doomed and damned, with no escape hatch, or with all the current criticism, at least, there must be an awareness by even the critics that without public schools as a viable option for all the people's children, the very fabric of the democratic system is at risk.

Public schools, with all their flaws, are the only place for the cultural universals of democracy to be implemented and practiced. Incapacitating and handicapping public schools will have the consequences of destroying the democratic ideal, that noble experiment that is increasingly becoming dysfunctional.

It is a failure of courage to withdraw from the system and assault it from outside, rather than work within the institution to improve it. Public schools cannot be made the scapegoat for poor parenting or lack of support from other institutions. Public schools cannot do everything.

Public schools get a bad press because of bad journalism. Too many journalists accentuate the negative and have an arrogant loathing of a nonelite education. Too many academicians, trained in intellectual ghettos of narrow specialization, have their axes to grind. But perhaps worst of all are the politicians who have made public schooling an arena for partisan political manipulation.

The schooling thrust today is one of quantification, technology, and the cognitive domain. Being an educated person is not dependent on what one knows but how one uses knowledge. Writing in 1955, Ralph Linton said, "Our preoccupation with technological development has led to a neglect of social invention which may well prove catastrophic."[1] Progress today is equated in terms of test taking, organization (longer day, year), time on task, and memorization, with little consideration for purpose and without consideration being given to the democratic context. The affective domain, ethics, problem solving, and higher order learning skills suffer neglect. These latter skills are not easily measured; accountability is not effective (or affective). Tragic is the belief that schooling and education are synonymous. Too frequently the creative, divergent student drops out of schooling—not just the public school. Schooling can get in the way of an education.

In order for this nation to long endure as a democracy, there must be a body of cultural universals as well as cultural alternatives. Only one American institution has the potential to perpetrate those cultural universals—the public schools.

Ralph Linton in *Study of Man* wrote:

> Without the backing of a group of like-minded people, it is impossible for him to feel absolutely sure about anything, and he falls prey to any sort of high-pressure propaganda.
>
> Such a condition is fatal to the effective operation of democratic institutions, since these depend upon a high degree of cultural participation, with the united will and consciousness of social as apart from individual interests which this confers.[2]

Only in the public schools can cultural pluralism, in a democratic sense, be implemented. To teach bilingual education as anything more than a transitional mechanism is to demean the very meaning of a democratic society. All subgroups must be responsible for contributions to the general welfare of the society. Cultural pluralism is a both-and proposition. It's a salad bowl, not an ice cube tray.

The public school system must go beyond the rhetoric of providing a general education for all future citizens[3] and devotion to the ideals of equality of opportunity and equality of status[4] as outlined by James B. Conant in 1959. There was a difference between his prescriptive values and his operational values. His twenty-one recommendations are essentially a multiplicity of techniques to segregate students within the comprehensive high school—grouping, grouping, grouping—when all the people's children were to be brought together under one roof. In spite of court decisions, homogeneous grouping continues to be typical of public schooling.

In McLaurin versus Okla. State Regents and Sweatt versus Painter (1950) the Supreme Court struck down state laws for the higher or professional education of Negroes as failing to meet the requirements of equality. Students who are segregated, grouped, have limitations placed on the opportunity to study, discuss, and exchange ideas—thereby inhibiting their growth professionally and educationally. In addition, the district court of Washington, D.C. in the Hansen versus Hobson case (1967) for all practical purposes declared tracking/homogeneous grouping unconstitutional. Even school board policy can establish a definitive threshold of learning for students. School boards, in some instances, have even determined what grades may be given students in certain groups.

Public schools to be public schools must provide an education for all students—regardless of sex, religion, national origin, race, or social class. In 1971, Michael Katz wrote: "My thesis is that by about 1880 American education had acquired its fundamental structural characteristics, and they have not altered since . . . It is, and was, universal, tax-supported, free, compulsory, *bureaucratic, racist,* and *class biased*" (italics added).[5]

In order for public schools to grow toward the democratic ideals, there must be community involvement. Information by school officials is not enough. There must be community participation in matters ranging from building programs and finance to curriculum development and in-service education. But responsible school officials dare not turn lay people loose—they must inform and explain, and they must take the risk of allowing lay groups to report their findings to the school board. To be effective, lay people must see their participation does make a difference.

References

1. Ralph Linton, *The Tree of Culture* (New York: Alfred A. Knopf, 1955), p. 52.
2. Ralph Linton, *The Study of Man*, 2d ed. (New York: Appleton-Century Company, 1936), p. 285.
3. James B. Conant, *The American High School Today: A First Report to Interested Citizens* (New York: McGraw-Hill Book Company, Inc., 1959), p. 17.
4. *Ibid*. p. 7.
5. Michael B. Katz, *Class, Bureaucracy, and Schools* (New York: Praeger Publishers, 1971), p. 59.

Cassandra's Crossing

PART I

THE THREAT

Chapter One

The Ideologues

To Kill a Goose*

I

In 1964 Dame Rebecca West raised a significant question regarding the relationship between a person and a nation-state. In The New Meaning of Treason, *she used Dr. Nunn May as a prime example of that postwar breed of scientists who claimed that because they were endowed with superior technical knowledge, they composed an elite that should be allowed to ignore national loyalties.*

II

At his inauguration, John F. Kennedy advised: "Ask not what your country can do for you; rather ask what you can do for your country." Then, the words rang true; now they seem hollow. America is adjective to everything these days: union, political party, religion, national origin. Everyone speaks of rights; no one speaks of responsibility.

The new generations of hyphenated Americans have lost their continuity with the past: They know not the struggle for freedom; they know only the sweet life. Except in the hinterlands and with the new immigrants, the virtues

*Originally published in *Contemporary Education* 58, no. 1 (Fall 1986), p. 5. Used by permission.

of patriotism, honesty, and trust have been replaced with selfishness, greed, and bigotry.

The decline of Rome was triggered by the barbarian invasion. Paradoxically, the American barbarians are the descendants of those who know the meaning of blood, toil, sweat, and tears.

Public schooling as a viable handmaiden to democracy is at a crossroads: Never before has there been such a plethora of criticism—mostly irresponsible, mostly with hidden agendas. Increasingly public schools have become a scapegoat for all of America's social problems.

The naive, the credulous, see the current spate of criticism as only being helpful—simply because attention is being paid to public schooling. The average citizen feels helpless, powerless when trying to make contact with the state or federal government or the bureaucracy, but average citizens can vent their frustrations at the local level and this can be helpful. But the danger lies in the distant power centers: *the news media* (it's monolithic), biased think tanks, ignorant governors, the U.S. Department of Education, knee-jerking congressional ideologues, and front organizations—the list goes on.

Walter Feinberg in a footnote to his preface in *Reason And Rhetoric* writes thusly: "Indeed there may be no more significant sign of the problems with our educational institutions, than the ease with which the centers of power can manipulate emotions to their own end."[1]

The criticism of public schooling is nothing new. The criticism is as old as the emergence of public schooling in this country. The early 1950s witnessed attacks on schools as being hotbeds of communism and un-Americanism. In Mary Anne Raywid's classic study *The Ax-Grinders: Critics of Our Public Schools,* she writes:

In this country there are approximately a thousand groups that are highly critical of public education. Yet even with a daily heightening of their vocalism in newspapers, books, and magazines, there persists the lethargic assumption that it is the sound of a noisy little group of disgruntled professors, publicists, and

4

admirals. But by virtue of numbers alone, the critics of educational policy and practice are a force to be reckoned with.[2]

She identifies a third of these critics as journalists and about a third as professors of liberal arts.[3]

What is so exacerbating is: What do journalists and liberal arts professors know about public schooling? Does one dare to ask the question: What are their credentials for writing and/or publishing/producing an exposé of public schooling? Are the only necessary credentials to belong to the right group or profess right thinking or to be the right kind of bigot? Is it not prerequisite that when one writes about a subject one should be knowledgeable about the subject?

Ronald G. Corwin writes:

> By virtue of their access to the media, certain television commentators have received more recognition as "educators" on public issues than university professors who have spent their lives studying and writing on the issues which news commentators dismiss in sixty-minute documentaries . . . these groups have assumed the authority to speak about issues that are beyond their demonstrated competence . . . this monopoly provides those in control with the power to exclude views unacceptable to them.[4]

But if one has docilely been indoctrinated in the classics, in the language, and in the arts, one has divine wisdom. They know because they know—they have so disciplined their intellect they can intuit the good, the true, the beautiful. Cute with words and articulate in literary allusions, how many of the so-called theoreticians have attended a public school (God save them from the unwashed bodies of the common people) or even entered the public school house door? Alas, some have dared to rub shoulders with the ordinary student, but their altruism lasts a year or two, and then they return to the airy ivory tower and write about their awful experience in public schools. It gives verification to their preconceived notion of how very bad public schools must be. And sometimes these critics are labeled as compassionate?

During the 1970s, the new criticism took on a new guise—"back to basics." But this was a "back to basics" with a difference:

> First, the new "back to basics" advocacy is not an internal conflict within the educational establishment . . . This movement is essentially a grass roots challenge by parents spearheaded by *non-school professionals* [italics added]—ministers, politicians, and leaders of community groups. Second, this is a movement without singular thrust and without organized and *identifiable* [italics added] leadership. Its concerns are many: textbooks, patriotism, discipline, morality, skill development—and it has assumed a variety of modes of operation: legislation, *propaganda* [italics added], intimidation, and harassment. Third, this back-to-basics call is meeting with success in state legislatures and school boards. Fourth, the back-to-basics emphasis of the mid-70s is emotion laden and tends toward ax-grinding. "Back to basics" reflects a growing frustration with bureaucracies, whether presidential, congressional, or educational.[5]

Robert C. Morris stated that the criticism in the late 1970s was different from that of the past. He wrote:

> Just as the critics of education during the McCarthy era varied widely on their "attacks" of public education, so today do the critics of our schools vary in their "criticisms." During the late 1940s and early 1950s, certain individuals and groups adopted demagogic and propagandistic methods, charging that educators had become "victims" of foreign ideologies and were engaged in attempts to subvert American youth to communistic and collectivistic ideas by means of new courses of study and group methods of instruction. Other critics of the day decried the "godless" schools, substandard education, educational frills, and socialistic if not communistic educational philosophy. Fault was found with both primary and secondary schools, with teachers, administrators, and finally with the archdemons of society, the professors of education. The chant went up that the schools were not doing their job.
> The allegations made by today's critics are quite similar to those earlier ones. The charges of obscenity, immorality, god-

6

lessness, and/or otherwise subversive nature in our schools' textbooks indicate a pattern not unlike the above-mentioned. These present day critics point to the quality of books read by the public, the prevalence of comic books as reading matter of the younger generation, corruption in Washington, athletic scandals, the high crime rate, the divorce situation, communism in government, and the poor intellectual quality of secondary and college students.[6]

In his personal correspondence with me (May 1988), Robert C. Morris, who has written extensively on the New Right, said:

Right-wing critics (individuals and organizations alike) often hide under the guise of a friendly interest in education, but in reality have been, and continue to be, actually attempting to undermine it. The critics' motives are seldom if ever clear to the outsider, but they seem to be actuated in part by a doubting attitude toward democracy and a desire to reduce the costs of public education. Some have even gone so far as to recommend the abolition of public schools and the placement of full responsibility for education on private institutions. The amount or extent of criticism, as well as the intensity of criticisms, fluctuates depending on the social scene and the current status of education, but overall activity and boldness of attack remain very much a part of American society. The perennial character of criticisms and of the nature of critics are facts that must always be kept in mind as one attempts to maintain balance and perspective when identifying and analyzing right-wing critics and their criticisms.

Ben Brodinsky sees an increase in the attack on public schools since the election of Ronald Reagan as president in 1980.[7] This can be explained partly by Reagan's espousal of many of the issues raised by the "New Right," for example, prayer in the school, tuition tax credits, and the dismantling of the U.S. Department of Education. These same critical groups, through the National Conservative Political Action Committee, were also able to aid in electing to Congress several candidates who support their causes.

No better example can be found of the right-wing ideologue and his threat to public schooling than the recent pronouncement of U.S. Education Secretary William Bennett. He was reported to have said in the Associated Press Newsfeatures as it appeared in the *Terre Haute Tribune-Star:* "Chicago's public schools are the worst in the nation and people raising families in the city should consider private education for their children. . . . The people who know the product [that's how he sees it] best send their children elsewhere."[8] He stressed the potential for government vouchers for private-school tuition. He said Chicago schools could "straighten up fast" through competition with private schools. The basis of his judgment: American College Test scores. (No hidden agenda here: It's on the table.)

Perhaps too much attention has been given to the right-wing ideologues and not enough to the left-wing ideologues. The left-wing ideologues are more difficult to confront: they are more surreptitious and clandestine; they criticize by innuendo, censor by benign neglect, intimidate by indirect, anonymous means—telephone calls, letters—even denying those with opposing views the opportunity to speak out, i.e., letters to editors and appearances in television discussions.

In an early paragraph of *A Nation At Risk* are these unforgettable words: "If an unfriendly foreign power had attempted to impose on America the mediocre educational performance that exists today, we might have viewed it as an act of war. As it stands, we have allowed this to happen to ourselves."[9]

However, the enemy is within. And the major enemy to public schooling is *the media,* television in particular and newspapers and news magazines as well.

Newspeak for 1988 often appears to have the following advocacy stances: Private and parochial schools are better than public; federal government is better than local; Democrats are more humane than Republicans; anyone west of the Appalachian Mountains is ignorant, disadvantaged; it's better to be Jewish or Catholic than Protestant; socialism is better than capitalism; and because they comprise an elite, the press should be allowed to ignore internal loyalties.

8

What the American public wants is not carefully monitored propaganda called the news—that is, information. The American public wants communication, evenhandedness, and less, much less, arrogance.

When approximately one-fourth of the American citizenry today are Hispanic and Black, people who are especially interested in public schooling and democracy, why are there so few Hispanic and Black journalists? Or writers of books? Why are some of the major commentators not even American citizens—and why are so many major commentators hyphenated-Americans, with *American* being the adjective?

A recent little volume by John Corry, a critic for the *New York Times,* is most telling. He admits that television does reflect a liberal or left point of view, but not consciously. He claims that it is an intellectual and artistic culture that shapes the journalists' assumptions.[10] And the intellectual and artistic culture is firmly rooted in the political left—where little dissent is tolerated. He notes incidentally that these journalists perhaps send their children to the better eastern schools.[11] This intellectual and artistic culture Corry calls the dominant culture (they control the perception)—and thereby they control the political and social environment.[12] Corry is forthright in stating that television rises above the national interest,[13] that television would find it unthinkable to rule out covering a victory parade over the United States.[14] Journalists encounter the feeling of the dominant culture that American life is rotten.[15] "Forget," Corry writes, "the free flow of ideas and a multiplicity of viewpoints; the dominant culture stands for no dissent."[16] "On respectable television news broadcasts, the word leftist is applied only to foreigners. Right wingers, on the other hand, are clearly identified."[17] Networks have increasingly come to not represent their country's interests, but their own interests, i.e., television.[18] The late Supreme Court justice Porter Stewart was reputed to have said that the press is the only private business given explicit constitutional protection.

Most of these left-wing critics, generation after generation, make clear they don't believe in democracy. They believe in that which is alien and ancient. H. G. Rickover, not noted for his humility, is symbolic of this kind of ideology. Writing in *American Education—A National Failure,* he notes: ". . . the Middle Ages have been bequeathed to the present an ideal of unity at the summit of man's intellectual potential, a readiness to emulate excellence as such, without reference to the nation where it comes into being."[19]

His methodology is simplistic and didactic. The principal task of the school, in his mind, is to develop the intellect—to transmit, as if by osmosis, a substantial body of knowledge to the student. Says he: "Many things are best learned through direct transmission from the mind of the teacher to the mind of the student without an intermediary stage of doing the things the teacher has been talking about."[20]

There is no better example of the foreign American than Allan Bloom. In Charles R. Kesler's review of *The Closing of the American Mind* he writes: "Bloom writes compellingly on Rousseau, Nietzsche, Flaubert, Goethe; but his references to the Founding Fathers are schematic at best. Washington, Hamilton, Jefferson, and Madison are simply invoked—or rather simply, as epigones of Hobbes and Locke. Like most of the superficial scholarship that he criticizes so eloquently, Bloom reduces the Founders to children of their age, of the Enlightenment."[21] And later Kesler writes: "Clearly Bloom's view of the American people is that they are even lower and less solid than they used to be. When it comes to handling serious German philosophy we are children playing with adult toys, it is all too much for us to handle. . . ."[22] And finally Kesler writes: "In nearly four hundred pages, Bloom does not mention even once the most famous of all attempts to educate the American mind—Jefferson's intricate blending of civic and philosophic education in his plan for the University of Virginia."[23]

James D. Koerner, the godfather of critics of public schooling, whose *The Miseducation of American Teachers* (1963) is still the handbook for contemporary soothsayers of doom and gloom in public schooling, uses a typical innuendo of the critics. He spends considerable time discussing the theory of Albert J. Nock, who was convinced that only a tiny minority of men were capable of education: The great majority of citizens should be given vocational training.

Then he quotes Nock as saying: " '[The] three most serious errors in the theory upon which the mechanics of our education were designed . . . were a fantastic and impracticable idea of equality, a fantastic and impracticable idea of democracy, and a fantastically exaggerated idea of the importance of literacy in assuring the support of a sound and enlightened public order.' "[24]

But, alas, Koerner asserts Nock was wrong! Koerner supports the idea of the great majority of people responding well to liberal education when it is conducted well. If it is not conducted well, whose fault is it?

And then if all else fails in attacking public schooling, they attack John Dewey, even when Mortimer Jerome Adler includes five of Dewey's books on his list of the greatest books of the twentieth century[25]: *Democracy and Education, Human Nature and Conduct, The Quest for Certainty, Experience and Nature,* and *Reconstruction in Philosophy,* and dedicates his *The Paideia Proposal: An Educational Manifesto* to Horace Mann, John Dewey, and Robert Hutchins[26]—men who Adler says would have been our leaders were they alive today.

All the ideologues would need to do is read John Dewey in the original, not from secondary or tertiary sources. No less than Sidney Hook in his essay "John Dewey and His Betrayers," writing in 1973, said that in the past the severest critics of public education came from the traditionalists who opposed the alleged inroads of progressive education on the curriculum, but the new wave of attacks "comes from those who regard themselves as libertarians and humanists and who profess themselves inspired to a considerable degree by the thought of John Dewey."[27]

Hook accused the radical romanticists of being intellectually irresponsible in disregarding and distorting Dewey's writings.

To the ideologues of the right and the left—who have found the answer—Dewey wrote in 1938:

> . . . those who are looking ahead to a new movement in education adapted to the existing need for a new social order should think

11

in terms of education itself rather than in terms of some ism about education, even such an ism as "progressivism." For in spite of itself any movement that thinks and acts in terms of an ism becomes so involved in reaction against other isms that it is unwittingly controlled by them. For it then forms the principles by reaction against them instead of by a comprehensive constructive survey of actual need, problems, and possibilities.[28]

Perhaps the ideologues who attack John Dewey do not have the patience to read first hand several of his significant books. Dewey's convoluted and careful language frustrates the ideologues. Perhaps no person other than the Christian's Christ has been so misinterpreted to serve selfish ends. The current best seller by E. D. Hirsch, Jr., is a classic example. It appears that Hirsch has read one of Dewey's earlier books, that is, *Schools of Tomorrow*, published in 1915. Four modest examples of Hirsch's misinterpretation of Dewey follow.

Hirsch writes: "In basic educational assumptions Dewey was a disciple of Rousseau."[29] Dewey was a disciple of no one, least of all Rousseau. Dewey's strength was his appropriation from a multiplicity of sources, such as Hegel, Mead, Pestalozzi, and others, and reconstructing, integrating their ideas into a new language—helping to create a uniquely American sociology, philosophy, and psychology. He redefines science, intelligence, religion, and democracy. He was criticized because he did not create a metaphysic. His intellectual thrust negates such a possibility. Naturally, the modern medieval minds have a mind-set against such thinking.

Hirsch also writes: "Dewey assumed that a child *would* become highly literate under his learning-by-doing principles of education."[30] Hirsch probably has confused William James with Dewey. Learning by experiencing, which Dewey believed in, is not the same as learning by doing. One of Dewey's major contributions to education is his concept of reflective thinking, which involves conjecturing consequences—mental testing before hypothesizing and overt action.

Hirsch also attributes to Dewey and Rousseau the following: "The new kind of teaching espoused by Rousseau and Dewey, which avoids rote learning . . ."[31]

"Espoused" is certainly the incorrect word to use regarding Dewey's philosophic stance, which was hypothetical. And Dewey never negated the importance of flexible drill. He would, of course, have been opposed to drill for drill's sake simply to discipline the intellect. To Dewey drill had to be purposeful, meaningful, and contextual.

Finally Hirsch writes that our elementary schools are dominated by the content-neutral ideas of Rousseau and Dewey.[32] He is wrong again. Dewey believed in teaching content, but he was also interested in the process. Hirsch, like so many of his clique, has been caught in the either-or-proposition; they cannot understand Dewey's both-and philosophy of enlargement, inclusiveness, and consensus.

What is most disturbing about Hirsch's book is the appendix. There are sixty-three pages of "terms-items" the literate American should know. Only six dates are listed, but such interesting selections as "vigilante," "nonperson," "nepotism," and "junta" are included. The interesting question is who is to play the philosopher king and determine what knowledge is of most worth *and to what depth.*

Hirsch echoes Philip H. Phenix with his definition of *architectonics:*

> The architectonics of knowledge has to do with the principles of ordering knowledge into systematic categories. Such an endeavor proceeds on the presupposition that knowledge has discriminable patterns or structures and that these structures can be organized according to some intelligible *master plan* [italics added].[33]

Or is Hirsch a disciple of Joseph T. Tykociner, who prefers zetetics? *Zetetics* is the science of research and artistic creation concerned with collecting and systematizing data on the theory and practice of zetesis, and aiming at the expansion and unification of knowledge into a *consistent system* [italics added].[34]

Oh, to be literate in the esoteric. . . .

What Dewey wrote in 1938 is even more appropriate in the 1980s. But what is to be done when 66 percent of Americans mention television as a main news source,[35] when 55 percent are inclined to believe television reports over newspapers, magazines, and radio?[36] The public does not believe in a centrally controlled media, whether by big government or big business. And it does not want a morally controlled media by self-appointed "guardians of the faith."[37]

As never before, there are alternative news sources—through cablevision. There are evenhanded approaches to news reporting. Americans need to become "active" rather than "passive" viewers. They need to read a variety of newspapers and magazines. If all else fails, there is an "off" button.

The fourth branch of government (who elected them!) finds the First Amendment sacrosanct, but it ignores the other first amendments, i.e., the Bill of Rights. The Seventh Amendment guarantees the right to trial by jury: Too often journalists act as jury and judge. The Fourth Amendment guarantees the right of people to be secure in their homes, papers, and effects: Too often journalists ignore the right of privacy. The Fifth Amendment guarantees that the right to life, liberty, and property cannot be taken away without due process: Too often journalists rush to judgment.

Unlike the president, the Congress, even the Supreme Court, journalists too often believe they are above the law. There are checks and balances for the legitimate branches of government. Even the courts are governed by judicial restraint, as articulated by Mr. Justice Brandeis. And the president and Congress must be evaluated by their constituency every two, four, or six years.

References

1. Walter Feinberg, *The Intellectual Foundations of Twentieth Century Liberal Educational Policy: Reason and Rhetoric* (New York: John Wiley and Sons, Inc., 1975), p. vi.

2. Mary Anne Raywid, *The Ax-Grinders: Critics of Our Public Schools* (New York: Macmillan, 1962), p. 3.
3. Ibid., p. 6.
4. Ronald G. Corwin, *A Sociology of Education: Emerging Patterns of Class, Status, and Power in the Public Schools* (New York: Appleton-Century-Crofts, 1965), pp. 225–26.
5. William Van Til, William E. Brownson, and Russell L. Hamm, "Back to Basics—With a Difference," *Educational Leadership* 33, no. 1 (October 1975), pp. 8–9. Reprinted with permission of the Association for Supervision and Curriculum Development. Copyright © by ASCD. All rights reserved.
6. Robert C. Morris, "The Right Wing Critics of Education: Yesterday and Today," *Educational Leadership* 35 (May 1978), pp. 628–29. Reprinted with permission of the Association for Supervision and Curriculum Development. Copyright © by ASCD. All rights reserved.
7. Ben Brodinsky, "The New Right: The Movement and Its Impact," *Phi Delta Kappan* 64 (October 1982), pp. 87–94.
8. Associated Press Newsfeatures in the *Tribune-Star* (Terre Haute, Indiana), Saturday, November 7, 1987, p. A5.
9. The National Commission on Excellence in Education, *A Nation At Risk: The Imperative for Educational Reform* (Washington, D.C.: U.S. Department of Education, April 1983), p. 5.
10. John Corry, *TV News and the Dominant Culture* (Washington, D.C.: Media Institute, 1986), p. 1.
11. Ibid., p. 19.
12. Ibid., p. 15.
13. Ibid., p. 33.
14. Ibid., p. 39.
15. Ibid., p. 19.
16. Ibid., p. 45.
17. Ibid., pp. 20–21.
18. Ibid., p. 26.
19. H. G. Rickover, *American Education: A National Failure* (New York: E. P. Dutton and Co., Inc., 1963), p. 126.
20. Ibid., p. 63.
21. Charles R. Kesler, "The Closing of Allan Bloom's Mind," *American Spectator* 20, no. 8 (August 1987), p. 15.
22. Ibid., p. 17.
23. Ibid.
24. Albert Jay Nock, *The Theory of Education in the United States* quoted in *The Miseducation of American Teachers* by James D. Koerner (Boston: Houghton Mifflin Company, 1963), p. 10.
25. "The Great Book (Contd.)," *Time*, March 7, 1977, pp. 65–66.
26. Mortimer J. Adler, *The Paideia Proposal: An Educational Manifesto*, (New York: Macmillan Publishing Co., Inc., 1982), p. v.
27. Sidney Hook, *Education and the Taming of Power* (La Salle, Ill.: Open Court, 1973), p. 89.
28. John Dewey, *Experience and Education* (New York: Macmillan, 1938), pp. vi–vii.
29. E. D. Hirsch, Jr., *Cultural Literacy: What Every American Needs to Know* (Boston: Houghton: Mifflin Company, 1987), p. 1.

30. Ibid., p. 122.
31. Ibid., p. 31.
32. Ibid., p. 19.
33. Philip H. Phenix, "The Architectonics of Knowledge," *Education and the Structure of Knowledge* (Chicago: Rand McNally and Company, 1964), p. 44.
34. Joseph T. Tykociner, "Zetetics and Areas of Knowledge" in *Education and the Structure of Knowledge* (Chicago: Rand McNally and Company, 1964), p. 123.
35. Robert E. Mulholland, *American's Watching: Public Attitudes Toward Television* (New York: 1987 Television Information Office/Roper Report), p. 4.
36. Ibid., p. 5.
37. Ibid., p. 11.

Chapter Two

The Bureaucrats

Teaching . . . 2021*

April 15, 2021

Dear Teresa:
   It is hard for me to understand that the art and the craft of teaching were not passed on to your generation. It was a practical knowledge that you can't get from a book. And what hurts most of all is the death of the humanistic traditions in education. Now teaching is such a piecemeal kind of thing. Teachers teach. Clerks clerk. Administrators administer. The teaching task, it now seems, is no more than specialized functions.
   I must be honest with you, Teresa; if I were choosing a career now it would not be teaching. The golden days are over. I wish I could help you with your concerns, but schools now, even the small ones, are simply bureaucracies. There is no one to listen to your concerns. There is no communication—only information. You and your students are not people anymore; you are simply cold, cognitive creatures trained in efficiency—no emotion, no caring, no self-actualization.
   Schools today are like factories. At a very early age the raw material is placed on the assembly line and each specialist does his minimal, specific task at each structured phase. One's existence matters only as it preserves the mega-machine.
   I sometimes wonder if I could have made a difference if I had spoken out, but I remained quiet. I saw the movement toward bigger is better, longer days

*Originally published in Contemporary Education 57, no. 4 (Summer 1986), p. 169. Used by permission.

and years, greater specialization, greater accountability, testing for evaluation, and rules, rules. . . . It's hard to escape from a climate of prudence and discretion, and words mean just the opposite of what they used to mean.

I guess I agree with Lewis Mumford. He wrote in The Pentagon of Power: *"Each one of us, as long as life stirs in him, may play a part in extricating himself from the power system by asserting his primacy as a person in quiet acts of mental or physical withdrawal—in gestures of nonconformity, in abstentions, restrictions, inhibitions, which will liberate him from the domination of the pentagon of power."*[1]

But enough of this. So good to hear from you. I love you so much. I wish you were here to see the fruit trees in bloom, the blue water, and the skies. And the quiet . . . oh, the wonderful quiet.

Love, your aunt,
Romana

When the idealism of an individual and/or group strives to carry out in practice the dogma, the ideology, of their belief system through a mechanistic means, a bureaucracy is in place. A current obscene example exists in Iran. It is the blending of the implicit with the explicit. Hitler's Germany was another classic example. There are examples, here and now, in the United States. The major purpose of a bureaucracy is to exert power over others, primarily through legalistic devices, red tape, and routine. Bureaucrats do not deal with people; they deal with functionaries. They are without intelligence or common sense; they are a new kind of being—unable to be empathic, caring, or understanding. They are interested in efficiency, accountability—seeing that bureaucracy itself survives, that and nothing more.

The bureaucratic system appears to be the panacea for those caught up in the so-called current effective school movement. There are specific behavioral objectives to be implemented with their concomitant specific outcomes. Information is compartmentalized in small units, and then the most efficient devices are applied to reinforce "positive" feedback. There is no place for divergent thinking, even the intuitive leap. It is a step-by-step procedure. And what does one do with the information? Bureaucrats believe information, specific facts, is enough. And alas, by rigorous testing one can quantify information, i.e., knowledge (synonymous?). To know the authors of books, the capitals of countries, and the spelling of difficult words does not bake bread in the real world. The effective school movement completely ignores the most important aspects of education, that is, critical thinking, problem solving, ethics, and creativity. Will the bureaucratic mentality admit that testing is not education? Will it admit that the most important element in schooling is education, not training? Will it admit that perhaps that wisest person is the one who knows how much is still unknown? Will it admit that no amount of information, knowledge, or skill can be isolated from the holistic nature of the human being? Without self-knowledge and increasing social-self realization, there is only the pompous ass, the emperor without new clothes. What good are hollow men with heads filled with isolated straws of facts when faced with a child's question? The most dangerous thing an educator can do in the 1980s is raise questions. But be it noted: there are no foolish questions, only foolish answers.

There is no better way to begin a discussion of the bureaucratic system than by referring to a one-page conversation with John Lukacs that appeared in *U.S. News and World Report* in 1984. He notes that the United States may have led the world into the democratic age, but that this may have been an episode and that the age of aristocracies may be followed by an age of bureaucracy, not democracy. He says the United States has been unable to avoid the degeneration of some of its institutions, and he sees the main source of this decay as the rise of bureaucracy and the bureaucratic mind. He writes:

> The inclination to administer, to standardize, to regulate, to reorganize, to define—and therefore constrict—personal activity and private choice is endemic in so-called private institutions, corporations, businesses as much as public ones.
>
> Bureaucratization is constricting not only our channels of production but those of our intellectual commerce.[2]

Bureaucracy and the bureaucratic mind are increasingly a

part of the education community—from local school corporations to large universities, from small elementary schools to large comprehensive high schools. And with the increasing governmental involvement with schooling there is the increasing influence and power of the bureaucracy.

There is an intimate relationship between power and bureaucracy. In his book *Power*, Adolf Berle wrote: "Top power holders must work through existing institutions perhaps extending or modifying them or must at once create new institutions. There is no other way of exercising power—unless it is limited to the range of the power holder's fist or his gun."[3] But that's the rub—modifying a bureaucracy. Berle further sees one of the great functions of bureaucracies as the continuity of government.[4]

Continuity is important, even essential, but if continuity is static, what price continuity?

Lewis Mumford in discussing the role of power points to an error made by the younger generation: "The notion that in order to avoid the predictable calamities that the power complex is bringing about, one must destroy the whole fabric of historic civilization and begin all over again on an entirely fresh foundation."[5]

The conundrum in dealing with bureaucracy is how to communicate, interact, and reconstruct. There is always the danger of being entrapped as a functionary, as a modular man—with the loss of identity, except as a part of the mega-machine. To be powerless is to be apathetic, to die (literally or figuratively), or to commit violence as a last resort.

In his introduction to *Future Shock* Alvin Toffler writes: "Earnest intellectuals talk bravely about 'educating change' or 'preparing for the future'. But we know virtually nothing about how to do it. In the most rapidly changing environment to which man has ever been exposed, we remain pitifully ignorant of how the human animal copes."[6] He says "we form limited involvement relationships with most of the people around us. Consciously or not, we define our relationships with most people in functional terms."[7]

In *Power and Innocence* Rollo May proposes that there are five levels of power present as potentialities in every human being's life. They range from the *power to be,* seen in the newborn infant; to *self-affirmation,* the cry for recognition; to *self-assertion,* overt "attention must be paid"; to *aggression,* moving into power positions/territory of another, taking over; and when all else fails, there is the ultimate explosion—*violence.*[8]

The seminal writing on bureaucracy was achieved by Max Weber in volume 3 of *Economy and Society: An Interpretive Sociology.* He explicitly outlines six characteristics of bureaucracy as paraphrased below:

1. Rules, laws, and administrative regulations provide official *jurisdictional areas* for action.[9]
2. *Office hierarchy* and channels of authority are systematized, with supervision of lower offices by higher offices.[10]
3. Management of the office is based upon *written documentation.*[11]
4. There is thorough training in a field of *specialization* in office management.[12]
5. Official activity demands *full working capacity* of the official.[13]
6. The management of the office follows *general rules,* stable and exhaustive, and knowledge of these rules represents technical expertise that the official possesses.[14]

Ralph P. Hummel in *The Bureaucratic Experience,* a modern classic on bureaucracy, gleaned from Weber's classic work (with extrapolations and with careful documentation), lists six more characteristics of bureaucracy.*

7. Human beings are treated/dealt with as cases; it "processes" only "cases."[15]
8. Man's social relations are converted into control relations.
9. Man's norms and beliefs concerning human ends are torn

*Except for characteristic 7, Hummel cites specific page numbers from *Economy and Society.* Characteristics 7 through 12 are paraphrased in a single paragraph on page 2 of *The Bureaucratic Experience.*

from him and replaced with skills affirming the ascendancy of technical means, whether of administration or production.

10. Psychologically, the new personality type is that of the rationalistic expert, incapable of emotion and devoid of will.
11. Language, once the means for bringing people into communications, becomes the secretive tool of one-way commands.
12. Politics, especially democratic politics, fades away as the method of publicly determining society wide goals based on human needs; it is replaced by administration.

Although Weber only devotes a few pages to bureaucracy and education, two other characteristics may be extracted:

13. A system of specialized examinations or tests of professional expertise are indispensable.[16]
14. The elaboration of diplomas from colleges and universities and the creation of further educational certificates serve the formation of a privileged stratum.[17]

Few social scientists have grappled with the problem of defining the *specific features of educational bureaucracy*. In 1935, Carl Joachim Friedrich outlined six features as follows:
1. There is centralization of control and supervision.
2. There is careful differentiation of duties for school functionaries.
3. There are definitive standards of certification and specific qualifications for office.
4. There is an emphasis on so-called objective measurement—for efficiency and economy.
5. There is further precision and consistency in hierarchy of line and staff.
6. Finally, there is a climate of prudence and discretion in an atmosphere of bureaucracy.[18]

Each of Friedrich's features will be further elaborated, one by one, to illustrate how public schools and districts have become, in far too many instances, mini-bureaucracies. Bureaucracy is a serious threat to the education of children and youth. Bureaucracy places democracy itself in *jeopardy*. The instrumentation of bureaucracy—computers, files, documents, policy statements—remain dormant until actualized by human intelligence. The words of Robert Penn Warren are haunting:

> One idea that seems painfully persuasive is that in the world of massive population and exploiting technology—in the technotronic age, as they call it—the boys who handle the post computer mechanism or who find themselves in charge of "conditioning" programs, will inevitably be in control—perhaps very high minded control—with a vast, functionless, pampered, and ultimately powerless population of nonexperts living on free time, unemployed and unemployable.[19]

Now to explicate Carl Friedrich's elements of bureaucracy in the real world of public schooling in the United States.

1. *There is a centralization of control and supervision.* Specific translation of this element into educational practice in the public schools centers on the concept that bigger is better. When James B. Conant wrote in *The American High School Today* that a high school must have a graduating class of at least one hundred students to function adequately as a comprehensive school, the consolidation bandwagon was set in motion.[20] Schools became too big. Students no longer had names, and they became lost in a mass of bodies. How right Ted Sizer was: Less is more. Big schools require more rules and guidelines in order to maintain control and order. It requires a greater number of controllers—a proliferated administrative staff dealing with specific operations of a large school. The ultimate is a central office building—remote from the everyday working of the school operation—distant bureaucrats who have no vista-vision (they are too specialized), and therefore many, many meetings of specialists to try to reach decisions, and this requires more and more paper trails of information. There must be standard oper-

ating procedures in place so that the supervisors can carry out the mission and follow the black book of school-board policy. And for consistency's sake, every possible contingency must be covered in policy. There must be *the* model of a good teacher, and supervisors must have an extensive form for quantitative "evaluation" of the teaching act. There must be *the* appropriate methodology. There must be testing, testing, testing of students to determine if they are meeting specific standards. Walk into the superintendent's office, and you will find the power positions carefully graphed on an organizational chart. It is generally framed and placed behind the superintendent's desk. And, too, you will find a map of the school district, also framed and strategically placed in the superintendent's office. The bureaucrat is interested in territoriality; the bigger the district, the bigger the school, the larger the pupil population, the more prestigious the functions of the multiplicity of controllers.

2. *There is careful differentiation of duties for school functionaries.* The school board policy handbook is filled with reams of job descriptions. No one is exempt from having a job description. (A humorous sidelight: A colleague once asked a janitor—whoops, maintenance engineer—if he could get his chalkboard washed. The next day a memo was found on his desk: "It's not in my job description.") There are not only job descriptions but policy as to grading, such as the highest or lowest grade that can be given a child in a certain designated group. There may be parking lot policy as to where students and faculty may park cars. Often the most powerful persons may have specially assigned parking spaces. Frequently the day begins with the morning announcements, such as: "Today we are on schedule 7, because of a special convocation. . . . Again I want to remind you of the policy with respect to the proper way to pull the window shades. I noted the variety of patterns this morning. It is not good public relations. Please note the new policy—6A-23 on dress codes. Students may wear blue jeans

on field trips with a parent's permission." There is policy such as standing by the door when classes are dismissed. There is policy as to the procedure of taking children in primary grades to the rest room.

3. *There are definitive standards of certification and specific qualifications for office.* Increasingly there are time constraints as to how long a college student is allowed to count courses for credit toward degree programs. Increasingly there are narrower and narrower certification requirements, with greater and greater specialization areas. Increasingly courses are being added—often with hidden prerequisites. Will the time come when one is specialized to teach only first grade or pre–Civil War American history in high school? To be a teacher and to continue to be one requires periodic testing, and many advanced degree programs require comprehensive evaluations or culminative experiences. Let it be clear: if this trend continues, smaller schools will have staffing problems and larger schools will have to cope with featherbedding. What is so frustrating is that there is generally conflict between the philosophy professed by state departments of education and what the operational requirements for certification are. And typically these bodies are unaware of this or choose to ignore it.

4. *There is an emphasis on so-called objective measurement—for efficiency and economy.* Essay exams are denigrated, because they are said to be too subjective. But is an objective test objective? Why are certain items chosen to the neglect of others? So-called objective tests do have the advantage of quick scoring and the opportunity to apply an array of statistics. Never mind that the most significant elements of an education cannot be tested on objective tests. And try this experiment: Give the same objective tests to the same group of students—six months later. I'll bet that many of the A students will flunk the exam the second time around. Objective testing encourages memorization, jumping over the hurdles, and low-level thinking. But that's what the bureaucrat wants—no thinking, just doing.

5. *There is further precision and consistency in a hierarchy of line and staff.* In a bureaucracy, the pecking order is made perfectly clear and the first lesson the novice must learn is what the channels of communication are! Many bureaucrats justify their existence by make-work: there is simply a flurry of forms to be filled out—in triplicate and duplicate. Today this is so well symbolized by so many so-called homerooms, which have simply become a place to fill out forms and listen to announcements—simply an administrative device. How well Bel Kaufman illustrated this memoranda mess in *Up the Down Staircase.*

6. *Finally, there is a climate of prudence and discretion in an atmosphere of bureaucracy.* Prudence is illustrated when people sitting in the lounge look around to see who is present before they speak. The bureaucrat notes when one arrives at school and when one leaves. In bureaucratic schools, attention will be paid to dress and grooming in specifics—men must wear ties, women dresses. One must attend the right churches and belong to the right clubs.

What, if anything, can be done to redirect the bureaucracy in the schools and the school districts? Theodore R. Sizer—in spite of his "elitist" educational background and in spite of an inappropriate title, "High School Reform: The Need for *Engineering*" (italics added)—in an article in the June 1983 issue of *Phi Delta Kappan* offers fourteen implicit suggestions. In summary, these recommendations are as follows: a shorter, simpler better-defined list of goals; concentration on reading, writing, and ciphering as prerequisite skills to further education; higher-order thinking skills; emphasis on learning (culminating experiences?); knowledge about knowledge; interdisciplinary experiences; slowing the pace; larger blocks of time; stopping age grading; lessening segregation by homogeneous grouping and tracking; out of school opportunities and less specialized teachers, that is, English and social studies may be taught by the same teacher; accommodations for individual differences; teacher autonomy; and differentiated staffing.[21]

What can be done about bureaucracy in the public schools? Below are an even dozen recommendations:

1. Staff the schools with empathic, caring people, who nonetheless set high standards for students. Since superintendents and principals set the psychological and social climate for a district or school, it is especially important that they have highly developed social skills.
2. In the administration of the schools, staff personnel—who work with teachers and others in nonthreatening ways—should be accentuated, while specialized line positions should be cut back or even eliminated.
3. Schools should be small enough so that the principal and teachers know the students as persons; smaller schools are more likely to develop an ethos, a feeling of belonging among the students and faculty.
4. All grouping by ability, that is, homogeneous grouping, should be eliminated. However, intraclass grouping related to skill development and special interests should be encouraged. Peer teaching can be effective, especially in group activity.
5. The school-board policy handbook should be reexamined to see if greater autonomy can be given principals, teachers, and students. Rules and regulations have proliferated unnecessarily in most school districts.
6. Evaluation of students and teachers should be emphasized rather than testing, testing, testing. There should be opportunities for student-teacher, parent-teacher conferences. Merit pay for teachers, if in place, should be eliminated; it is a vehicle for competition and divisiveness among all school personnel.
7. All courses in the curriculum should be vocational. For example, English courses should teach students how to read, write, listen . . . rather than to diagram sentences and underline subjects and predicates. History courses should be about issues, and dialogue and discussion should replace lecture. And for some students, distributive education, art,

music, and physical education are of more worth than the so-called academic subjects.

8. There should be in-service education for teachers and staff at least once monthly—during the school day—where questions and problems of mutual interest can be discussed. The key purpose of in-service education should be curricular reconstruction for the local district rather than appropriating systematic prepackaged programs.

9. School districts should provide for teacher and pupil governance, such as faculty councils and student councils. The publication of a newsletter can provide a good means of communication among teachers.

10. School organization should provide for large blocks of time where interdisciplinary teaching can occur. The boundary lines between content fields should be broken down. Even science and English teachers can cooperatively work together on science projects.

11. Too much emphasis has been given to technology. Incorrect use of computers, programmed instruction, and films can create distance between students and teacher.

12. Eliminate the unnecessary number of forms, which take time away from teaching. This is especially true in special education. Some teachers spend more time with paperwork than they do working with children.

And why is bureaucracy a threat to public schooling? Jack Frymeir states it well:

> But there are many people in policy-making roles and administrative positions who mouth pat phrases about the importance of teachers and teaching—and then proceed to undercut teachers by creating conditions of work that blunt their enthusiasm and stifle their creativity. I see such actions as a kind of "neutering" of teachers. Neutered teachers lack physical strength and energy, enthusiasm for their work, and motivation. For teachers, motivation is as important as cognitive and professional skills . . .[22]

He goes on to write: "In the main, the bureaucratic structure of the work place is more influential in determining what professionals do than are personal abilities, professional training, or previous experience. Therefore, change efforts should focus on the structure of the workplace, not on the teachers."[23] As he says, the bureaucratic nature of the educational enterprise seems to have acquired a purpose all its own. The current educational panacea, the effective school movement, facilitates the bureaucratic system.

References

1. Lewis Mumford, *The Myth in the Machine: The Pentagon of Power* (New York: Harcourt, Brace, Jovanovich, Inc:, 1970), p. 433.
2. John Lukacs, "The Age of Bureaucracy Has Replaced the Era of Democracy," *U.S. News and World Report* 97, (August 13, 1984), p. 70.
3. Adolph A. Berle, *Power* (New York: Harcourt, Brace, and World, Inc., 1969), pp. 92–315 passim.
4. Ibid., p. 318.
5. Lewis Mumford, op cit. p. 404.
6. Alvin Toffler, *Future Shock* (New York: Random House, 1970), p. 4.
7. Ibid., p. 87.
8. Rollo May, *Power and Innocence: A Search for the Source of Violence* (New York: W. W. Norton and Company, Inc., 1972), pp. 40–43.
9. Max Weber, *Economy and Society: An Outline of Interpretative Sociology,* vol. 3, ed. Guenther Roth and Claus Wittick trans.: Ephraim Fischoff et al., (New York: Bedminster Press, 1968), p. 956.
10. Ibid., p. 957.
11. Ibid.
12. Ibid., p. 958.
13. Ibid.
14. Ibid.
15. Ralph P. Hummel, *The Bureaucratic Experience* (New York: St. Martin's Press, 1977), p. 25.
16. Max Weber, op. cit., p. 999.
17. Ibid., p. 1000.
18. Carl Joachim Friedrich, "Responsible Government Service Under the American Constitution," in *Problems of the American Public Service: Five Monographs on Specific Aspects of Personnel Administration* (New York: McGraw-Hill Book Company, Inc., 1935), p. 29.

19. Robert Penn Warren, "There is Real Danger of Dictational Power," *U.S. News and World Report* 79 (July 7, 1975), p. 48.
20. James B. Conant, *The American High School Today: A Report to Interested Citizens* (New York: McGraw-Hill Book Company, Inc., 1959), p. 14.
21. Theodore R. Sizer, "High School Reform: The Need for Engineering," *Phi Delta Kappan* 64, no. 10 (June 1983), pp. 682–83.
22. Jack Frymier, "Bureaucracy and the Neutering of Teachers," *Phi Delta Kappan* 69, no. 1 (September 1987), p. 9.
23. Ibid., p. 10.

Chapter Three

The Politicians

To Murder or Create*

Children and youth are dying daily in classrooms across the country. I write not of quietus, but of apathy. Joy, excitement, emotion have gone out of learning; these creatures of blood and flesh move as automatons—listening to dry voices, shuffling sere foolscaps, and mumbling the catechism of inanity.

Immobile they sit, watching the clock, daring not to question, to digress. They envy the butterfly that creeps across the windowpane—autonomous in its small way. For the butterfly is alive to sun, air, and wind.

They sit and stare—already dropouts to learning, even to human contact. For their day is measured out with the rituals of bells, lines, forms, and tests.

To be creative is to copy. To be intelligent is to quote. To enjoy is to pantomime.

The tragedy is that murderers are ignorant of their crimes, and they will go unpunished. At least the ancient Spartans let their children die in peace.

Politicians, let our children go.

Nothing can be more detrimental to the future of public schooling than for the institution to become a political football. And so it has become. Schooling, education perhaps, may be a major—if not the major—issue in the upcoming presidential and congressional elections.

The GOP, in this decade, appears to support private and

*Originally published in *Contemporary Education* 59, no. 4 (Summer 1988), p. 189. Used by permission.

parochial schools over public schools. They seem to support the laissez-faire, free-market approach to schooling that was in vogue a hundred years ago. They generally are in favor of the voucher system (an administrative nightmare) and tuition tax credits. The agenda is not that hidden.

The Democrats, on the other hand, appear to support massive amounts of funding (with accountability—especially categorical aid with implicit controls). Democrats have little faith in local school boards. The hidden agenda of the Democrats is a federal system of public schooling.

In appealing to the special interests, the left-wingers who support private schooling and the right-wingers who support Christian schooling, these presidential candidates have not taken time to consider the effect these strategies would have upon public schooling. Don't forget for a moment that who controls the honey (special interest groups) controls the bees (the politicians). Unfortunately, American politicians, with few exceptions, have been bought and paid for. They seek power, and to achieve power a politician has to be elected, and that requires massive amounts of money.

Mr. DuPont, born with a silver spoon in his mouth, wants the individual states to provide parental choice—and competition in all elementary and secondary schools. It can only be assumed that elitist institutions—the best money can buy—would compete with disadvantaged rural and inner-city ghetto schools that are getting by on shoestring budgets. But, oh, yes, there is the voucher system (and private and parochial schools can't be made to participate)—and, of course, gerrymandering can be applied to public schools. Haven't DuPont and his proponents ever heard of the bad days at Alum Rock, the experiment that failed? It included just public schools within the poor, largely minority-student school district. The voucher system raises the specter of economic and racial segregation.

R. Freeman Butts, noted educational historian, states the case well. He says: "I believe a full-scale voucher scheme will promote *private* purposes rather than *public* purpose."[1]

Being an historian, Butts takes us back to the early nineteenth century:

> Then . . . many kinds of attempts were made to channel funds into the charity schools, the denominational schools, the private academies, and the philanthropic societies; and in the emerging public schools "rate bills" were levied upon parents who could afford to pay, while "free schooling" was often reserved for the poor. All in all, the diversity and the use of public funds for private purpose approached the situation to which present-day voucher schemes might very well return us.[2]

Rep. Jack Kemp of New York is pushing a proposal to teach foreign language as early as kindergarten. Is that the knowledge of most worth to children at this age and stage of development? Even the Latin grammar school of the seventeenth century didn't start Latin and Greek at that early age. What foreign language?

But as David Elkind has written: "In America, educational practice is determined by economic, political, and social considerations much more than it is by what we know about what constitutes good pedagogy for children."[3]

Dr. Elkind goes on to point out the short-term and long-term risks of too early introduction to formal instruction. Among the short-term risks is stress. The several long-term risks are potential harm to the child's motivation—dependency on adult direction, social risk, and intellectual risk.[4]

Alexander Haig favors national teacher certification and a "core curriculum." Haig's "core curriculum" probably harks back to the recommendations, for secondary and elementary schools respectively, by the Committee of Ten (1883) and the Committee of Fifteen (1895). He also wants schools to teach "virtues not just values"—whatever that means. Senator Dole falls back on the old saw: "Education is a national concern, a state responsibility and a local function."

Democrats, on the other hand, put their faith in increasing federal aid to education. Perhaps Congressman Richard Gephardt's proposal among the Democrats is most frightening. He would reward school districts that show the most improvement. The flaw to Gephardt's plan is obvious. Good districts would become better, while poor districts would become even worse off. His carrot and stick approach, of course, would be federal aid.

But, as usual, Democrats believe the way to solve the problems of public schooling is to spend, spend, spend—even after the experience of the Johnson era. The Democrats would make public schools houses of ill repute; the oldest and second oldest professions would merge. They are raping public schools through misguided humanism—humanism at a distance!

Not since the immediate decades before the War between the States has there been such focus on education by leaders in the individual states. During that era the leaders were Horace Mann of Massachusetts, Henry Barnard of Connecticut and Rhode Island, Caleb Mills of Indiana, Robert J. Breckinridge of Kentucky, Calvin Stowe of Ohio . . . and the list goes on. These men were educators in the true sense—men of good intent, supportive of education for the common man. But today, paradoxically, the so-called leaders in education from the individual states are governors. George R. Kaplan cites a corps of current and recent "education" governors whose commitment to schools and teachers has been extraordinary.[5] Or so he says! Practitioners in the field—the front line forces—would generally not agree. Many of the governor's proposals are counterproductive to intent, and sometimes the high sounding motives are highly suspect. Perhaps the highest qualification of the governors is that in some instances they may have attended a public school. How many of these governors have been "professionals" in the field of education? To be blunt, most have simply gotten on the anti–public school bandwagon. Being political animals, they are dedicated first of all to getting reelected or keeping their party in power. Commitment to private and parochial schools? Commitment to harassment of teachers and administrators through more demands, more requirements, more competency testing, more merit pay, more accountability? Commitment to children in making demands and requirements beyond their developmental level, pressuring them into dropping out, alienation, suicide, and violence. What arrogance! What ignorance!

To politicize public schooling will be disastrous, because there are no quick-fix, simplistic answers. The greatest danger to public schooling is the instant expert with the latest panacea—*who* pontificates with witticism—the usual, that is, "form without substance."

To be governor appears to be more important than what is best for children and youth. Governors, with their limited terms of office, don't have to live with the consequences of their impulsive acts. *They don't have to live with the consequences of the damage they do to human beings who are vulnerable to their scapegoating.* A good analogy is to warmongering old men in high places who send "invisible" young men off to war. Governors who have the answers ought to be required to spend just one week *in a public school classroom.* As those in the "profession" facetiously say, it would be a learning experience. Governor Orr is noted for his perfunctory visitations to classrooms with the television cameras whirring. Thomas Kean of New Jersey should spend a week as an administrator of a public school, since he thinks no training skills in school administration are necessary. Lamar Alexander of Tennessee should investigate the morale of teachers in Tennessee as a result of his innovation.

Item

Governor Thomas H. Kean in a speech before a joint session of the legislature September 6, 1983, said, "The way we certify teachers actively discourages talent from entering the profession. I see glaring need to open the profession to otherwise highly qualified candidates who have not taken courses in education. For instance, there are many people now teaching in private and parochial schools who would rather teach in public schools, but will not go back to college to take education courses which they consider meaningless."[6] By the same logic, the legal and medical profession should be opened to talented people who would not have to bother with the special skills needed to advise clients or diagnose patients. He also shows his not so hidden agenda in referring to teachers in private and parochial schools who would rather teach in public schools. Why?

Item

In Tennessee there is Lamar Alexander's Career Ladders. In "Career Ladder Plans: Trends and Emerging Issues," it is noted that the Tennessee Career Plan was one of the first state-wide plans to be funded and implemented. The brochure states:

> In the first year of implementation of the Tennessee Career Ladder Program, 39,800 teachers and administrators—about 92 percent of those eligible by virtue of having at least three years of experience—have *voluntarily* [italics added] entered the new certification program. The state evaluated 3,120 candidates for the upper career levels. The State Board of Education recently announced that 458 teachers have attained Career Level II status; 632 attained Career Level III. With those certificates come state-paid incentive supplements ranging from $2,000 to $7,000 and additional professional opportunities including extended contracts and new responsibilities. In addition, 148 administrators attained career level certification at the upper levels.[7]

One might well ask when teachers have time to teach and plan with such a bureaucracy in place. Oh, yes, what about the morale of teachers—especially if they are labeled low-level?

Item

In Indiana there is Gov. Robert Orr and PRIME TIME. In a memorandum from Joe Di Laura, director of Communications,

Indiana Department of Public Instruction, is the following definition of PRIME TIME.

> PRIME TIME is a unique approach to state funding of elementary education. Under the provisions of the legislation, the state will reimburse local districts the costs of hiring teachers to teach class sections of 18 or fewer students. The law authorizes $18,000 per teacher hired. The program ultimately will cover the first four grades (K-3) and will be phased in one grade per year for the next four years. For the 1984–85 school year, first grade will be implemented, then followed by second, third, and kindergarten in succeeding years.[8]

Be it noted the experimental pilot programs had a student-teacher ratio of 14 to 1, with the follow-up and research conducted by the Department of Public Instruction. The legislation also gives school districts that are strapped for space an opportunity to participate in the program through the hiring of certified teacher aides. Common sense would indicate only smaller classes would be more effective—right? But what if the teacher taught 18 students the same way he or she taught twenty-five students? And how far is the follow-through going to continue? Also, note that the legislature established a student competency testing and remediation program that would begin in the spring of 1985 with the testing of third-graders. Is the new trend testing, not teaching?

And then there are the teachers' unions. Let them be called what they really are. It was the National Education Association that endorsed Democrats in the last three presidential elections. It was the lobbying of the NEA that obtained the cabinet office Secretary of Education. It is only justice that now the organization has William Bennett as Secretary of Education.

Unfortunately, teachers' unions have narrowed their membership to the proletariat of product sellers. With few exceptions (lifetime membership), administrators and professors cannot belong to the unions. The philosophy of the union is them against us. No longer is there dialogue or listening. Now it's "professional negotiations" or "professional sanctions," but

37

now bluntly called collective bargaining and teacher's strikes. Strikes are called primarily for higher salaries and better working conditions—and their union responsibilities to children and the community are afterthoughts. Quickly unions have taken over the characteristics of bureaucracies: decision making is highly decentralized; work, that is, teaching, has become increasingly specialized and task oriented; the master contract has become the standard of performance. And the hierarchy, not the figureheads, of the unions often are not teachers but bureaucrats.

Now the teaching proletariat sees the enemy not only as administrators, but board members, college professors, the lay public—and too often the students. No wonder the public is becoming increasingly disenchanted with unionism.

Perhaps there is no group more naive about politics than teachers. As a result, they have become stalking horses for the rich politicians who operate in the shadows. The hidden persuaders (a term coined by Vance Packard) are the producers of television programs and the editors and publishers of magazines and newspapers and books. Unless the message fits the particular political bias of the power brokers, it will not be published or produced. And if the message "does make it" in some obscure way, then the power brokers will censor by benign neglect.

Public school educators are rarely regarded as leaders in U.S. society, and never are elementary or secondary teachers so regarded.[9] Who creates the image of "leaders"? The anti–public schooling media gives "air-time" primarily to those ideologues who are sure to lambaste public schooling. On occasion, token time is given to a public school person, if the deck is carefully stacked.

When George R. Kaplan includes Gregory Anrig as one of the Big Four educational leaders, the nadir has been reached. Who is he? He is head of the Educational Testing Service. Has he ever been a public school administrator or teacher? What are his credentials? Kaplan writes that "under Anrig's *management* [italics added] and *leadership* [italics added] ETS has been both cost-effective and competitive." While in the past, according to Kaplan: "Like many too many educational organizations, gov-

38

ernmental bureaucracies, hospitals, the Educational Testing Service had drifted into a preoccupation with internal organizational interests at the expense of clients and customers."[10]

Another so-called educational leader listed by Kaplan is Albert Shanker, the president of the American Federation of Teachers since 1974. Why not the president of the NEA, the larger union? Or Secretary of Education William Bennett? Could it be because Shanker's views are compatible with the hidden agenda? Kaplan admits: "His views usually have the backing of the largely urban AFT membership, even when their connection to pedagogy is extremely tenuous."[11]

Or even more telling: "Nothing galls the Shanker conscience more than a system in which prescriptions for daily professional performance come from administrators and not from teachers themselves."[12]

Current politicians seem to be following the advice of Diogenes of Sinope: "Why not whip the teacher when the pupil misbehaves?" At the same time, politicians need to take a long, hard look in the mirror and reexamine what appears to be the common sense approach to improving public schooling. Common sense is never simplistic or expedient. René Descartes thought: "Common sense is the best distributed commodity in the world, for every man is convinced that he is well supplied with it."

What to do? Teachers, administrators, and the public must become better informed about politicians. They must take seriously the responsibility for casting intelligent, thoughtful votes at local, state, and national elections. They must think not only of what's best for them, but what is best for all the people in this democratic society.

References

1. R. Freeman Butts, "Educational Vouchers: The Private Pursuit of the Public Purse," *Phi Delta Kappan* 61, no. 1 (September 1979), p. 7.
2. Ibid., p. 8.

3. David Elkind, "Formal Education and Early Childhood Education: An Essential Difference," *Phi Delta Kappan* 67, no. 9 (May 1986), p. 632.
4. Ibid., pp. 634–36.
5. George R. Kaplan, "Shining Lights in High Places: Education's Top Four Leaders and Their Heirs," *Phi Delta Kappan* 67, no. 1 (September 1985), p. 15.
6. Governor Thomas H. Kean, "Education in New Jersey: A Blueprint for Reform" (Speech before a joint session of the legislature, September 6, 1983, mimeographed), pp. 15–16.
7. Lynn Cornett and Karen Weeks, "Career Ladder Plans: Trends and Emerging Issues," *Career Ladder Clearinghouse*, July 1985, p. 22.
8. State of Indiana, Department of Public Instruction, Division of Communication, State House, Indianapolis, June 1, 1984, p. 1, passim.
9. Dennis P. Doyle and Terry W. Hartle, "Leadership in Education: Governors, Legislators, and Teachers," *Phi Delta Kappan* 67, no. 1 (September 1985), pp. 21–22.
10. Kaplan, op. cit., p. 9.
11. Ibid., p. 13.
12. Ibid.

PART II

THE HOPE

Chapter Four

The Administrator

The Bare Bodkin*

The reports, the critiques, and the recommendations on how to improve (?) public schooling (education?) have essentially ignored the necessary catalyst for that improvement—the educational leader—be he or she a superintendent, principal, or other administrator.

And there's the rub. The centerpiece to public school administration dysfunction is too often the flagrant violation of a basic principle: Public schools are to reflect a democratic society. Too often the public school administrator supervises rather than counsels, informs rather than communicates, creates a climate of prudence and discretion rather than a climate for exploration, discovery, and learning—and teachers and students become functionaries, cases, no longer persons.

A corollary dysfunction is that too often public school administrators assume change is progress. There is little concern for assumptions—sociological, psychological—or concern for possible consequences for implementation of so-called innovations. No matter if it's simply a new name for an old panacea that failed—20 years ago, 40 years ago—no matter if it violates equal opportunity, due process—and that the hidden agenda may be even racist or sexist.

Most frightening of all, public school administrators increasingly are obsessed with instrumental goals and values, with the concomitant outcomes of greed, competition, and self-serving, backbiting cliques. . . . The code words for these accelerating instrumental goals are time-on-task, behavioral objectives,

*Originally published in *Contemporary Education* 57, no. 2 (Winter 1986), p. 65. Used by permission.

minimum competency, mastery learning, accountability, and programmatic budgeting. . . . Public schools are becoming more bureaucratic, inflexible, systematized, organized—factories for indoctrination.

But this is the caveat: for every action there is a reaction, not only in physics but in human relations. The history of American education is replete with examples of its dialectical nature.

There is a quiet revolution brewing out there. Those common sense folks are unhappy with public schooling, but are the managers, the budgeteers, the programmers listening? Perhaps, the patrons, parents, are saying, "The experts, those with a microcosmic view, are the ones who know least about public schooling. Hey, you, it's not your school, not your teachers; it's our school. And damn it, we have something to say about it. That's one place at least where we can still raise hell."

A critical, if not crucial, factor in the survival of the public schools as the safety net for democracy in the United States is the superintendent and the principal. The key element of their roles is whether they will be educational leaders in more than theory. They must be alive to the overwhelming influence they have on the students, the teachers, the staff. They establish the climate—psychologically, sociologically, economically, philosophically. If they see their role as only that of manager, expediter, supervisor, or book man, that is, the bureaucrat, the public schools can only get worse. He or she must first of all be an expert in human relations and have social intelligence and common sense. If the administrator respects human beings as persons first and as teachers, students, and staff personnel second, he or she will be able to set the stage for excellence. People strive to live up to expectations. If the administrator views the faculty as excellent, they will attempt to live up to that perception. If the administrator views the students as talented and gifted, they will try to fulfill those expectations.

The importance of the administrator is well documented in the literature. Ernest Boyer devotes a chapter in his book *High School: A Report on Secondary Education in America* to the principal as leader. Even though Boyer notes the difficulty of the principal becoming a catalyst, a change agent, there is still—even today—much "wiggle room" and opportunity to give teachers greater autonomy. As Boyer writes: "Today, most principals are caught in a complicated bureaucratic web. Far too many of our school systems are top heavy with administration; they are administered to within an inch of their lives. School leadership is crippled by layer upon layer of administration."[1] An alternative exists: In the line-staff organization, line personnel should be cut back drastically and replaced with staff personnel, that is, consultants and coordinators, who can work with teachers in a nonthreatening and helpful way. In addition, administration responsibilities should be integrated; there is far too much specialization. Frankly, a school and a district can be more effective if the now proliferated administration personnel are drastically cut and roles are multidimensional. For example, a curriculum coordinator would be involved in the hiring process, the "supervision" of beginning teachers, in-service and staff development, testing, and evaluation, as well as curriculum development. A job description based on this philosophy is as follows:

Coordinator of Curriculum and Instruction K–12

1. With the help of the teachers, principals and special personnel, to organize and develop curriculum studies and to prepare curriculum bulletins and materials. (This would include registration bulletins, summer school bulletins, et cetera.)
2. With the help of the teachers, principals, and special personnel, to maintain articulation of the curriculum between grades and between the school levels, kindergarten, elementary, junior high, and senior high.
3. To work with the principals in evaluating the curriculum experiences of the students both within and outside the classrooms of the schools.
4. To help orient new teachers to the school system in basic district philosophy, in lesson planning, and in instructional procedures. (This would require actual visitation to the

classroom and conferences with the teachers.)
5. Upon request (of the superintendent or principal) to aid experienced teachers with instructional procedures.
6. To work with teachers, principals, and parents to aid experienced teachers with instructional procedures.
7. To develop and coordinate in-service training activities and programs. (More opportunity must be provided through early dismissal time when teachers teaching in the same content fields [7–12] may meet together to discuss curriculum, tests, and instructional problems.)
8. With the help and advice of principals and teachers, to recommend textbooks for adoption. (A procedure for addition, change, or deletion of courses should be developed.)
9. To organize and coordinate with the approval of the superintendent and school board necessary research on educational methods and materials (K–12).
10. To work with the guidance staff in administering and evaluating the testing program (K–12).
11. To coordinate the placement of student teachers with the principals and regular classroom instructors affected (K–12).
12. To coordinate and centralize the procedures for hiring new teaching personnel. Whenever possible, the principals of the schools should be involved in the selections process.
13. To review orders for instructional materials to ensure uniformity with regard to district adoptions and policy. (An immediate concern should be the publication of a textbook order and inventory form. The form not only will be used for ordering purposes, but list books on hand and date of publication.)
14. To organize and direct summer remedial or enrichment instructional programs.
15. To prepare for the use of the principal's lists of substitute teachers.

Boyer also believes "that principals and staffs of individual schools need far more autonomy and authority to carry out their responsibility. Heavy doses of bureaucracy are stifling creativity in too many schools, and preventing principals and their staffs from exercising their best professional judgment on decisions that should be made at the local level."[2] To hypothesize from a distance is dangerous. School clientele and personnel differ. The administration must learn the local community—the social class, racial, and ethnic power configurations—by experiencing them, not theorizing about them.

Boyer is supported by other perceptive educators like John Goodlad: "There is no educating of young people in the school system; it takes place in terms of thousands of individual schools. Reconstruction must take place, then, in each of these schools, one by one, by the people who live and work in them and by those who send their children to them. Any overhaul of the system must be directed to increasing its ability to provide services to each local school."[3]

This is in marked contrast to E. D. Hirsch, an ideologue who bemoans the fragmentation of American education: "Our elementary schools are . . . governed by approximately sixteen thousand independent school districts . . . this dispersion of educational authority [is] an unsurmountable obstacle to altering the fragmentation of the school curriculum . . ."[4]

One can only assume that Hirsch would prefer a national curriculum that exists in some of the authoritarian nations throughout the world, where the Minister of Education can check the time and know what page is being studied throughout the nation state and of course the chosen few, like him, would make the decision as to what specifics would be taught, to whom, and when.

John I. Goodlad in *A Place Called School: Prospects for the Future* also points to the important role of the principal:

> Principals of schools that teachers found "more satisfying" felt themselves to be more significantly in control of their jobs and use of time and to have more influence over decisions regarding their own schools than did principals of schools perceived by teachers as "less satisfying." Without exception, the principals of the most satisfying schools saw the amount of influence they had as congruent with the amount of influence they thought principals should have.[5]

Goodlad cautions that it is simplistic to attribute "everything" to the quality of the principal's leadership role. (It's just as simplistic to attribute all of the ills of public schools to the quality of teachers. What about the quality of parenting? Quality of students? Quality of Congress and state legislatures?) Nonetheless, too little attention has been given to the important role the superintendent and the principal play "for better or for worse" in the educational setting. If an educator truly wants to make an impact on public schools, the best way to do so is to become a superintendent or principal, not a college professor, a writer of books or grants, or a researcher.

Too frequently courses required as qualifications for positions such as superintendent or principal, that is, courses such as Legal Aspects of School Administration, School-Community Relations, Educational Facility Planning, School Business Administration, and Public School Finance, are denigrated by "outside experts" who have never been administrators. Practical courses of this kind are essential to being successful as an administrator. The plague of public schools is administrators who are academicians. They cannot be bothered by the nitty-gritty of seeing that a school runs, or as far as that goes, they cannot be bothered by people. They prefer artifacts. But charisma and charades will play in Peoria for only the honeymoon.

One of the best public administrators I ever saw in action was a physical education major. Curtis Johnson, now deceased, once president of NASSP, knew how to hire quality people and then free them to do their best. He was often out of his office "getting the lay of the land" and "seeing what was happening." Sometimes he would engage a few students in the hallway, and take them to his office to talk. He was always available to teachers and other school personnel. He was at school early and stayed late—he was at athletic events, PTA meetings, and school plays, taking pride in the success of teachers and students. He knew people's names and, oh, yes, he even spoke to people in the hallway and the lounge. Incidentally, Alexander Ramsey, where Curt was principal, was one of the schools Conant visited in the late 1950s.

The very core of the administrator's education is the internship. Suddenly one does not move from being a teacher—or, God help us, a businessman—to becoming a principal. There is the "hidden curriculum" that is not to be found in textbooks. There needs to be a gradual transition to the principalship or superintendency. Otherwise, there may be "reality shock" or the administrator may find himself "a sociological stranger" in his own school and his own community. He must see the importance of the interdependence and interrelationship of the entire population. The janitor and cafeteria manager are just as important as the business manager and administrative assistant. The handicapped child and the disadvantaged child are just as important as the varsity football player and the valedictorian. And no one, not even the philosopher king, can live without a support system. There is no greater loneliness than to be lost in a crowd of strange faces.

How often I've seen administrator's personalities change when they became administrators. A little bit of authority "went to their heads." They would only socialize with those they considered their equals. And how quickly they were able to surround themselves with sycophants, who would tell them what they wanted to hear. As a result, the faculty formed into cliques and factions. There were designations like "the fair-haired boy," "the queen bee syndrome," and so on. The administrator must not lose perspective, even though some teachers and students begin to act and react to him/her differently with the new title. (Plato escaped from Syracuse with stealth.) Everyone needs to recognize that they are no better and no less than anyone else. Everyone is a human being who lives on borrowed time, rented land. Whoever flaunts his/her superiority only exhibits inferiority.

Today [writes Toffler] I believe we stand on the edge of a new age of synthesis. In all intellectual fields, from the hard sciences to sociology, psychology, and economics, especially economics—we are likely to see a return to larger-scale thinking, to general theory, to the putting of the pieces back together again.

For it is beginning to dawn on us that our obsessive emphasis on quantified detail without context, or progressively finer and fewer measurement of smaller problems, leaves us knowing more and more about less and less.[6]

The question is: Will school administrators prepare themselves to continue to be educational leaders for a new age, and will they have the courage and commitment to stand firm for children, for teachers, and for their public against the ultra-conservatives of the right and the demagogues (demigods) of the left? It will not be easy.

In 1978, Maggie Carey and I wrote an article in the NASSP Bulletin in which we said:

. . . the changing social scene requires new roles for administrators: the spotlight must also focus on additional goals and functions in the educational process.

Since futurologists predict that schools will continue to provide alternatives for students and their parents, and since students and parents play an increasing role in decision making about educational matters, school administrators must undergo a role transformation not only with respect to their clientele, but also in their relationships with teachers, counselors, and other school personnel. In fact, students, teachers, and school personnel require of administrators a different operational stance. There will be different role expectations and there will be different aspects to self-actualization. Each administrator must be cognizant of his leadership function, and of his interactions with people in fulfilling this function.

Those school administrators who commit themselves to "the bigger the better" philosophy are inevitably doomed to administrative dysfunction. This can be illustrated in the emphasis given ends over means, in the priority given practical operations over theoretical assumptions, and finally in the thrust of control and accountability over creativity and freedom. Specific examples of dysfunction can be provided by examining the five S's of school administration, five assumed goods: Specialization, Systemization, Socialization, Synchronization and Saturation.

Specialization

The unique specializations of teachers need to be exploited; but, carried to extremes, this can bring about student-student, teacher-student, even administrative-teacher isolation and segregation. A mathematics teacher, for example, may be caught up in his specialty to the extent that he has little patience with slower students and abhors so-called basic courses. He may become obsessed with teaching mathematics—not students. An administrator, too, can become such a specialist (as a specialist in federal programs) that his specialty becomes his main concern, to the exclusion of all others.

Systemization

Without order and systemization, pandemonium reigns; yet scheduling and programming can become so efficient that the human element is excluded. In the less systemized, computerized days of administering schools, principals knew students and teachers well enough to carefully match them. Bus routes were reviewed by the school superintendent with attention to the safety and convenience of students. The superintendent knew the buildings and grounds of his district intimately. He knew which rooms might have a heating problem, which teachers required larger rooms, which teachers needed encouragement and praise. With today's large numbers of students, the emphasis is on efficiency and economy. System and order have become the watchwords of educational administration. There is an atmosphere of mechanization.

Socialization

The increasing emphasis given to socialization and adjustment of students to the school environment would seem to be a happy circumstance. It would seem that schools are becoming more humanized; that a humanistic, interactive relationship was developing among the various facets of the school community. But wait! John Goodlad, among others, warns us that it is our responsibility to assist the learner in becoming more adaptable rather than in becoming adapted to a fixed order.

However, in some schools, students have become institutionalized. They are forced to fit a particular mold. They are expected to take on a certain "ethos" of the school. There is little self-actualization or social self-realization. The students simply fall prey to conformity—they do what is expected of them.

Synchronization

Synchronization refers to curricular processes—to vertical and horizontal articulation. However, in the eagerness of school administrators to facilitate the necessary scope and sequence in curricula, this attempt at articulation comes from the top down and becomes prescribed. A research study regarding teachers' perceptions of how curricular decisions should be made indicates that such decisions ought to be made either by majority vote of teachers and principals or by the principal with significant input from teachers.*

When the administrator prescribes curriculum, individual teachers lose their individual teaching styles; they become inhibited, and boredom frequently follows.

Synchronization can also refer to scheduling—as in modular scheduling, or doing away with bells. The bells may ring in the student's heads at more frequent intervals, and modular scheduling, which was introduced to provide greater flexibility, may result in a more rigid framework.

*ERIC: Information from the Clearing House on Educational Management, "What Do You Know About Curriculum Decision Making?" NASSP Bulletin 60, no. 402 (October 1976), pp. 108–110.

Saturation

Saturation has to do with obsession of administrators to get it all in. It goes something like this: With the rapid and often unpredictable changes and expansion in knowledge, how will it be possible to cover the material? (Never asking if it is desirable to teach everything!) So, the curriculum expands, expands, expands. Nothing is deleted. By creating semester courses, by expanding the school day and year, by shortening the class period, by adding minicourses, students are encouraged, even required to take more and more course work. Of course, it is desirable that schools provide a curriculum where students will be challenged, where they can test themselves. However, this can go too far.

Students ought not to be cheated out of childhood and youth by being bogged down with homework, projects, and reading until their whole life is school. No wonder more and more students are "dropping off" the educational ladder.

School administrators are in the best possible position for real educational leadership. They, however, must exercise caution. It is possible that a good idea can be overworked. A school administrator needs to consider alternatives, to be aware of implications and consequences. Most importantly, the school administrator needs to be aware that administration is a function of many people, not of any particular individual. Dysfunction can be avoided by viewing specialization, systemization, socialization, synchronization, and saturation from a multi-faceted perspective. The school administrator's lifestyle is one of hypotheses, not certainties.[7]

It is fascinating to note that Alvin Toffler in *The Third Wave* (1980) pointed to the rules or principles that run through every civilization like a repeated design. (Note: The Second Wave of change was touched off by the Industrial Revolution.) The Second Wave principles he describes are standardization, specialization, synchronization, concentration, maximization, and centralization.[8] The reader will note the similarity of these principles to the Carey-Hamm principles—that could cause school administration to become dysfunctional.

This is the time for school administrators to strive for a new leadership style that accentuates human relations and community relations, that accentuates quality over quantity, that accentuates cooperation rather than competition, that accentuates communication over information, and that accentuates their responsible role model for integrity, honesty, loyalty, and openness in public schooling.

References

1. Ernest L. Boyer, *High School: A Report on Secondary Education in America* (New York: Harper and Row, 1983), p. 234.
2. Ibid., p. 227.
3. John Goodlad, "Schooling Issues and Answers," *St.Louis Post-Dispatch*, Special magazine section: "Ideals in Transition: Tomorrow's America," March 25, 1979, p. 72.
4. E. D. Hirsch, Jr., *Cultural Literacy: What Every American Needs to Know* (Boston: Houghton-Mifflin Company, 1987), p. 19.
5. John L. Goodlad, *A Place Called School: Prospects for the Future* (New York: McGraw-Hill Book Company, 1984), p. 179.
6. Alvin Toffler, *The Third Wave* (New York: William Morrow and Company, Inc., 1980), p. 120.
7. Maggie Carey and Russell Hamm, "Dysfunction in School Administration," *NASSP Bulletin* 62, no. 415 (February 1978), pp. 1–4. Reprinted by permission of the *NASSP Bulletin* and Maggie Carey, Acting Assistant Superintendent, Educational Instructional Services, Gary (Indiana) Community Schools.
8. Alvin Toffler, op. cit., pp. 39–53

Chapter Five

The Teacher

Teaching as Learning*

I

A college professor was reputed to have said: "Teaching would be great if it weren't for the damned students." Perhaps we in higher education have forgotten our primary mission—the education of students. Too often the college teacher who neglects to do research, to get grants, or to write but rather concentrates on teaching is often denigrated, considered a second-class colleague or even a dunce.

But research cannot be conducted in a vacuum, or grants written devoid of interest, or professional writing done without "firing line" experience. Perhaps teaching is prerequisite to "having arrived" in the upper class of the academic community.

To know is not enough in order to teach. To inform is not to teach. There must be listening, active interaction in the dialogue. Teaching is not the dry echo of one's own voice.

The damned students are important if one dares to open up one's own assumptions for examinations. A different perspective, a change of view, can bring new life into teaching—and into research, grantsmanship, and writing.

It was a child who said the emperor wears no clothes. Are we naked?

II

Central to the troubles and to the solution are the professors, for the development that overwhelmed the old curriculum and changed the entire nature of higher education was the transformation of the professors from teachers concerned with characters and minds of their students to profes-

*Originally published in *Contemporary Education* 56, no. 2 (Summer 1985), p. 201. Used by permission.

55

sionals, scholars with Ph.D. degrees with an allegiance to academic disciplines stronger than their commitment to teaching or to the life of the institutions where they are employed. As appropriate as research is as the focus of energies and resources in the research university, the exclusive concern with research in the training of recipients of the Ph.D. degree—to the neglect of any concern with teaching or with any professional responsibility other than to scholarship—has encouraged college faculties to abandon the sense of corporate responsibility that characterized professors of the pre-professional era.[1]

Students and teachers in the classroom—that's where the action is. If that setting is dysfunctional, everything else is dysfunctional. Even George F. Will has written: "Between us and that night [transmission of the achievements of the giants of other generations] stands a thin line of the best teachers."[2] This, he writes, is the season to honor those teachers who do not produce "flat-souled" pupils. I couldn't agree more. Then why don't he and his ilk get off teachers' backs and let them do their job? It is the propaganda of the ideologies of the right and left that have created the perception that there are no good teachers out there in public schools, and that perception has become the reality.

It was centuries ago that Seneca said, "It is when the gods hate a man with uncommon abhorrence that they drive him into the profession of a schoolmaster."

A casual acquaintance with the reality of teaching in the public schools today reveals a disenchantment. Teachers are leaving the profession in droves, with their idealism shattered. Too often the ones who leave the profession are the creative, the brightest and the best, because they require autonomy. And because of the increasing policy mandates—state and local—many teachers complain they spend more time with paperwork than with people. Often they are held accountable for matters over which they have no control. There is frustration and anger among many teaching staffs and this affects their pupils as well.

After having spent my professional career in the classroom, I would have to give serious consideration to becoming a teacher again, if possible. There is too much competition, too much backbiting, too much attention to material things rather than to human beings. And if human beings are considered, they are cases, not people with feelings and needs. The obsession with the cognitive domain—especially with the testing mania—has caused teachers to become purveyors of information. Only the brave teacher deals with higher-order thinking or controversial topics: There is always someone listening in; there is always someone there to keep order and control.

Unlike the critics, having visited hundreds and hundreds of public school classrooms over two score of years as supervisor of students, coordinator of curriculum, and evaluator, without equivocation I can report that the very best "teaching" occurs in the elementary classrooms and the very worst occurs at the college and university levels. And one would assume the very opposite would be true. But it seems that the more knowledgeable, the more specialized the instructor, the least able the instructor is "to get across" to students. Of course, there is a caveat: college and university students are lucky to have a distinguished educator; instead they get a harried graduate student while the professor is writing grants, doing research, or on a lecture circuit.

Elementary teachers, be it noted, get their "training" essentially in schools of education by so-called educationists, the bane of critics, while in high schools the overwhelming number of hours of course work are taken in liberal arts. There is an old saw: teachers teach as they have been taught. Perhaps the greatest crisis in public schooling is to get the liberal arts professors to meet their first responsibility of doing the very best job they can as teachers—that's what they are paid to do! Perhaps I'm naive, but I thought college and universities existed primarily for students.

In a keynote address before a conference co-sponsored by Educational Facilities Laboratories and the Institute for Development of Educational Activities, Inc., Harold Howe II said, ". . . those who work with older students might learn a number of lessons from the elementary school. Among the most important is the role of the teacher. In too many secondary schools the teacher engages far too much of the time in what I have described as 'frontal teaching . . .' "[3] On the other hand, he sees a "well-run open classroom in elementary school" as being "a beehive of activity. Students are engaged in a variety of projects. Students are learning from the teacher, from books, from each other, from manipulating all sorts of materials, from planning and carrying through projects. In the midst of all this the teacher is helper, asker of questions, diagnostician of an individual youngster's learning problems. The planning time and observation skills required of the teacher are most demanding."[4]

Howe notes that translating this type of approach to the high school is not a simple task, but he refers to documented successful efforts to duplicate this process in a little book called *Intraclass Grouping in the Secondary School*. The author of this little volume outlines eleven characteristics of intraclass grouping and insists it is not just small group instruction but instead is a student-oriented innovation. The process helps students to define problems that are significant and interesting, asks critical questions, and places the major emphasis on making learning vocational and functional.[5]

Somewhere in the intermediate grades, the children begin to lose their enthusiasm for learning, their curiosity, and their excitement. They stop asking those wonderful questions. My hypothesis is that it's about the time—with the pushing down of content, especially with the middle school concept—that the process of education is replaced with the product of education. Children are cheated out of childhood and made to conform to unnatural developmental patterns. That's when the institutionalization process begins.

After all the tirades by critics, after all the reports, after all the politicking, it comes down to this: The heart of the teaching-learning experience occurs in the individual classroom across the country. And it matters not what the physical facilities are—it could be a barn (the ancients, like Socrates, even used the street). The teacher is key. How successful the teacher is depends on how he/she is able to adjust and cope with the increasingly diversified student population. And there is not *the* methodology of doing it. There is not *the* curriculum that will do it. Elementary

58

and junior high school teachers are more adept at using a variety of methodologies and teaching styles, and they even have greater opportunity to do interdisciplinary, cooperative teaching. (Note: I didn't say team teaching.) Far too many secondary schools and almost all college and university teachers use the sterile, didactic methods, centuries old, of lecturing, reading frayed notes, or, yes, even reading the textbook to students. If many secondary teachers teach this way, if most of their course work is in liberal arts, who are their models?

Perhaps the greatest myth perpetuated by the uninformed is that there is a good teacher. Who is a good teacher? Much depends upon your philosophical-sociological-psychological bias. People who should know better have implemented merit pay, career ladders, or master teacher programs. The assumption is that there is a *definite* definition of a good teacher. (Socrates took the hemlock because he was corrupting youth; that is, he was making questioners of his clientele. Today the brightest and best of our young teachers are leaving in droves because they cannot tolerate the dehumanization and head games of the bureaucracy.) Ask any student at random who a good teacher is. He or she will tell you, first, the teacher has a passion for teaching, has feelings for people, listens and discusses, and has humility about truth. (A wise man is an ignorant man thinking; so Socrates was reputed to have said.)

It follows that if a good teacher can be defined, then a training regime can be systematized to achieve a fault-free model. But it would seem that even the most unsophisticated layman would note that every person is unique, no two of a kind.

If people are unique, if teachers are unique—surprise!—then the goal of teacher education, not training, ought to be to free teachers and thus free students to discover their own idiosyncratic way of learning. That assumes that teachers need the autonomy to try out, to explore, and to discover what is most effective for them. There is no growth without risk taking or the opportunity to profit by acknowledgment of mistakes. In his foreword to *The Trail to Crazy Man*, Louis L. Amour is on target.

Although he was writing about becoming a good writer, his advice applies to teaching as well. One does not suddenly become a good teacher. Teaching skills must be sharpened and developed by practice—no matter how much innate talent the teacher has. A [teacher] never knows enough; a teacher is never good enough.[6]

And add to this what Thoreau said in *Walden:* "Perhaps the facts most astounding and most real are never communicated by man to man."[7]

What knowledge is of most worth for teacher education—or any education? How carefully the critics ignore the most significant piece of research having to do with students' success in higher education. It flies in the face of everything the critics would have secondary schools do today. It flies in the face of the foreign Americans' ideas of what *the* curriculum should be. How many of these demagogues have ever heard of *The Eight Year Study?* A résumé of that study follows.

Perhaps the most significant piece of educational research ever conducted in the United States was the Eight-Year Study. In May 1932, about three hundred American college and universities agreed to a proposal from the Commission on the Relation of School and College of the Progressive Education Association that thirty selected secondary schools should be set free by the colleges from the usual program of colleges' prerequisites to engage in experimental study of secondary education. The colleges agreed to consider for acceptance students from these schools for a period of five years, starting in 1936, without further examination and without regard to course and unit requirements then generally in force.[8]

The thirty schools chosen appeared willing and able to conduct exploratory studies and make creative changes in the secondary-school curriculum. The changes began in 1933. The commission *did not prescribe a curriculum to be tested.* Each school determined what changes should be made in the curriculum in view of the *special needs of its students and the community.*

Although evaluation was an ongoing process from the beginning of the experiment, the second phase of the evaluation took place in the colleges. Each graduate of the Thirty Schools was *very carefully* matched with another student in the same college who had graduated from a school not in the Eight-Year Study and thus had met the usual entrance requirements. A total of 1,475 matched pairs of students were studied.[9]

Among the eighteen general findings of the study were the following. The graduates of the Thirty Schools:

earned a slightly higher total grade average;
earned higher grade averages in all subject fields except foreign
   language;
received slightly more academic honors in each year;
were more often judged to possess a high degree of intellectual
   curiosity and drive;
were more often judged to be precise, systematic, and objective
   in their thinking;
more often demonstrated a high degree of resourcefulness in
   meeting new situations;
participated somewhat more frequently and more often enjoyed
   appreciative experiences in the arts;
participated more in all organized students' groups except religious and "service" activities;
earned in each college year a higher percentage of nonacademic
   honors;
had a somewhat better orientation toward the choice of a vo-
   cation; and
demonstrated a more active concern for what was going on in
   the world.

As stated in the study:

   It is quite obvious from these data that the Thirty Schools
   graduates, as a group, have done a somewhat better job than the
   comparison group whether success is judged by college standards, by the students' contemporaries, or by the individual students.
   The Thirty Schools differed widely in the extent to which
   they experimented. A special analysis was . . . made of the grad-

uates of the six schools whose programs differed most sharply from the conventional. The graduates of the most experimental schools were strikingly more successful than their matchees. Differences in their favor were much greater than the differences between the total Thirty Schools and their comparison group. . . .

A study was made of the graduates of two schools which were among the most progressive. . . . The superiority of these progressive graduates over their comparison group was greater than any previous differences reported.

Clearly, among the Thirty Schools, the more experimental the school, the greater the success in college. Furthermore, although students of high aptitude seem to have profited most from experimental education, students of low aptitude profited as much from experimental programs as their matches did from conventional schooling.[10]

The implications of this study are self-evident to anyone except the ideologues of the right or left.

The reason teachers fail—those who are dismissed or those still on the job—is not because they lack knowledge of subject matter. Those teachers who fail, fail because they cannot get along with students, colleagues, administrators, or parents. They fail because they have no self-knowledge either. No less than Charles Silberman, a journalist, in *Crisis in the Classroom* wrote that perhaps the "most neglected" aspect of teacher education is "helping the prospective teacher understand *himself.*"[11]

Only as a person grows in self-knowledge and self-understanding, can one begin to know "the other," the people with whom he/she works. As he/she grows in self-understanding, the more he/she comes to know strengths and weaknesses, and he/she will be better able to cope with all the anxieties, fears, and frustrations that exist in a school setting. With self-understanding, the teacher is less likely to fall prey to taking himself/herself too seriously and become too concerned with students liking him/her. Poise and confidence come only with self-understanding.

How should teachers be educated, according to Silberman?

"Teacher education has suffered too long from too many answers and too few questions. After all the dashed hopes of the postwar period it may be time to worry less about finding the right answers and more about asking the right questions."[12] What is the central purpose of teacher education, according to Silberman?

> . . . to provide teachers with a sense of purpose, or, if you will, with a philosophy of education. This means developing teachers' ability and their desire to think seriously, deeply, and continuously about the purposes and consequences of what they do—about the ways in which their curriculum and teaching methods, classroom and school organization, testing and grading procedures, affect purpose and are affected by it.[13]

The classic statement from *Crisis in the Classroom* is as follows:

> . . . teachers need more than a knowledge of subject matter and a little practice teaching experience before they enter the classroom. They need knowledge about knowledge, about the ramifications of the subject or subjects they teach, about how those subjects relate to other subjects and to knowledge—and life—in general. They need understanding of the processes of growth and development and of the nature of mind and thought. Most important, perhaps, they need to know that they need to know these things—they need to understand the kinds of questions their teaching will raise and to have some sense of where to turn for further understanding.[14]

And let this be clear. There is no way that any curriculum can provide everything a teacher needs to know. It is important that the teacher needs to know *how much there is to know*, to appreciate his or her own ignorance. It is important that teachers be turned on to the excitement of holistic living . . . to continue to read, to experiment, to explore. As Dewey put it, growth is far more growth. Change itself is the only absolute.

During the last three decades, professionalism has taken on

a new meaning, and this new stance may be counterproductive to the status of teachers and the best interests of public schooling. Too many teachers confuse teacher organizations with professional organizations.

Ronald G. Corwin, writing in 1965, said: "A professional is responsible for the individual welfare of his clients and he focuses on their unique problems."[15] But Corwin also notes that increasing class sizes and the standardizing of courses and examinations are practices that "explicitly ignore the personalities of students."[16] Increasingly there is a public perception that teachers are not primarily interested in the well-being of students but are more interested in increased salaries and better working conditions. In a more recent book Corwin writes: "The burgeoning teacher organizations provide the basis for *institutionalizing* conflict, especially in the forms of collective bargaining and binding arbitration."[17] He also notes that "the scope of bargaining also has been considerably broadened to encompass practically every problem that teachers might encounter, including not only wages, hours and conditions of work, and class size but also making education policy as well."[18]

This raises the very serious question as to who should make policy in a democratic society—and for public schools! Is policy to be made by lay school boards or by teachers' unions? Or by the staff members of professional organizations?

Myron Lieberman in an article written for *Phi Delta Kappan* in 1971 indicates even at that time the number of full-time professional staff members had increased tenfold.[19] He also notes that the teacher negotiating teams are increasingly dominated by full-time professional staffs. The professional staff members are providing the political clout that teacher organizations lacked in the past.[20] Just who are these staff members? Have they been teachers? Are they knowledgeable about public schooling?

Teacher organizations have become increasingly involved with partisan politics. The teacher organizations are now perceived as a political force in the Democratic party. In the last three presidential elections, they have supported the Democrat, and the Democrat has lost. Obviously many teachers voted against the wishes of their(?) organization. The stature of teachers has suffered because of their increased militancy. The unionization of teachers and especially the use of strike have denigrated the image of teachers. It is a public demonstration of their priorities. To put it bluntly: A professional does not strike. A professional *earns* the designation not by confrontation, but by proving to parents and lay people in the community that he or she is doing the best possible "job." Increasingly the climate for learning in public schools has been harmed by the infighting between teachers, administrators, school board members, and parents. The interactions between the parties have become depersonalized; there is less dialogue and discussion; there is less "ethos" and greater alienation, particularly for the young people who are caught in the crossfire of the power struggle.

Teachers are wont to say, "We deserve a living wage." True, but that's getting the cart before the horse. Too frequently teachers who are trying their best in the most difficult of situations are laughed at and even ridiculed by colleagues who put in their time and just get by: "You're making us look bad." Perhaps that's why some of the brightest and best of those who become teachers burn out or drop out quickly. Their idealistic image of what a professional should be is soon tarnished.

Corwin in *Education in Crisis* contracts bureaucratic and professional-employee principles of organization. He believes "there are three points of conflict between bureaucratic and professional principles: (1) the form of specialization, (2) the way work is regulated, and (3) the decision making process."[21] Bureaucrats specialize in particular tasks and techniques, as (in the extreme) on the factory assembly line.[22] Bureaucrats believe in standardization. Bureaucrats believe in centralization. As Corwin says: "In bureaucratic organizations, one derives his authority primarily from the *position* [italics added] that he holds."[23] Using Corwin's schema, a case can easily be made that organizationally, at least, public schools are increasingly bureaucratic and do not operate on professional-employee principles.

If you are a teacher, remember this: you are not *just a teacher!*

Your potential for good or evil is too awful to be taken lightly. Go therefore with courage and commitment, even as a voice in the wilderness, even now as stranger in your own country. Who knows but what happens in your individual classroom can be a positive virus that can become an epidemic?

The most serious question each individual teacher must face in the 1980s is: Just what does it mean to be a professional?

References

1. Association of American Colleges Committee, "Integrity in the College Curriculum," *Chronicle of Higher Education* 88, February 13, 1985, p. 14.
2. George F. Will, "Learning from the Giants," *Newsweek* 110, no. 11 (September 14, 1987), p. 96.
3. Harold Howe II, Keynote Address, "How You Gonna Keep 'em Down at the School after They've Seen T.V." in *The Greening of the High School: A Report on a Conference* (New York: Educational Facilities Laboratories, Inc. 1973), pp. 78–87.
4. Ibid., p. 85.
5. Russell L. Hamm, *Intraclass Grouping in the Secondary Schools* (Danville, Ill: Interstate Printers and Publishers, 1971), pp. 3–10.
6. Louis L. Amour, *The Trail to Crazy Man* (New York: Bantam Books, 1986), p. viii.
7. Henry David Thoreau, *Walden*, ed. Basil Willey (New York: Bramhall House, 1951), p. 236.
8. Dean Chamberlain, Enid Chamberlain, Neal E. Drought, and William E. Scott, *Did They Succeed in College: The Follow-Up Study of the Graduates of the Thirty Schools* (New York: McGraw-Hill, 1988).
9. Ibid., pp. 207–209.
10. Ibid.
11. Charles E. Silberman, "The Education of Educators," in *Crisis in the Classroom, The Remaking of American Education* (New York: Random House, 1970), p. 494.
12. Ibid., p. 471.
13. Ibid., p. 472.
14. Ibid., pp. 489–90.
15. Ronald G. Corwin, *A Sociology of Education* (New York: Appleton-Century Crofts, 1965), p. 231.
16. Ibid.
17. Ronald G. Corwin, *Education in Crisis: A Sociological Analysis of Schools and Universities in Transition* (New York: John Wiley and Sons, Inc., 1974), p. 230.
18. Ibid.

19. Myron Lieberman, "The Future of Collective Negotiations," *Phi Delta Kappan* 53 (December 1971), p. 214.
20. Ibid., p. 215.
21. Ronald G. Corwin, *Education in Crisis*, op. cit., p. 246.
22. Ibid.
23. Ibid., p. 248.

Chapter Six

The Public

The Public

Walden XIII*

It was 7:06 A.M. at the Farmers' Cafe, River City, Indiana—and it was raining. Eight men, most in bib overalls, were lounging around a large oval table at the front of the restaurant—sipping coffee, reading newspapers, magazines.

Charlie Yonts's stabbing finger got everyone's attention. He was pointing to a chart in a tattered newsmagazine. "It says here that marrieds are down and singles are up. Just more news that this country is going to hell in a handbasket."

Wanda Bryce, whose husband had left for parts unknown—leaving her with two preschoolers, was moving about the table refilling the coffee cups. With a wry smile she said: "It seems to me, Charlie, that if you were such a family man you would be home with your little wife and kids having breakfast with them—not that I'm discouraging business. But knowing you, I'd be surprised if you didn't demand breakfast in bed."

Briefly taken aback, he blurted out: "You gals just don't seem to understand that men are predisposed to run in packs—got to have these get-togethers . . . it's genetics. . . ."

*Originally published in Contemporary Education 57, no. 1 (Fall 1985), p. 53. Used by permission.

Farley McGee, a wizened seventy-six, hammered the ashes out of his pipe. His voice had a burr to it. "Charlie, are you trying to make out I'm some kind of deviate 'cause I divorced my first wife all those years ago, and you folks all treated me like I wore skunk spray for years? Always did beat around the bush, Charlie."

Charlie, always the gadfly: " 'Member when they had that whoop-te-do conference back in Washington few years back—couldn't even agree on what a family was. Damn it, kids need family."

Bruce McCall, a dropout from State University, always red-faced and the youngest of the bunch, cut in: "You miss the point. Some families are hell to live in—all kinds of abuse, and psychological the worst, the scars are hidden. Maybe something went wrong with the thing called family. And Farley was a man before his time."

Hal McNaughty, in a booming voice: "I've been married to the old woman for forty years, raised six kids. . . ."

Farley interrupted, "But you're never home, Hal. You didn't raise 'em. Your wife did. That's what I call a one-parent home. You just greased 'em and turned 'em loose." There was feigned laughter.

Slim Wilkins, fortyish and shy, almost whispered. . . . "I keep trying; I just can't stand to live alone. I can't hack it. And I tell you there's problems. . . . There's Jenny's kids, my kids, and our kid . . . complicated business tryin' not to show favorites. . . . Farley may have cut the first furrow, but plowing the whole field is wearing me out."

Bill Boscow, massaging his coffee cup and very deliberate, broke in: "Raising kids wasn't all that complicated a few years back before the '60s when they had chores, things to do at home, but now nobody knows for sure how to do it—least of all those experts down at State University. Far as I'm concerned, the real expert on growing is Granny Brown. . . . Her prescription is plenty of love and attention and experience! Having been there."

Charlie couldn't contain himself anymore. "It's those damned drugs and promiscuity. This suicide among kids really hurts me. Some of those wild-eyed crusaders on the bomb and acid rain, whatever . . . ought to see what the real problem is: human conservation . . . and it starts at home."

Wanda, pale and trying to make it sound funny: "Any you guys know a man who makes forty thousand dollars a year who's looking for a hardworking, love-starved woman, with two kids . . . who would jump at the chance to be just a housewife. You can't live on love, boys. . . ."

Farley could hear his own breathing. Time was a cornfield in August. Who would have the courage to break the pall of silence? Even the rain was silent on the windowpane. Somehow it reminded Slim of teardrops.

Why public schools? To serve the public's interests is the quick answer. But what are the public's interests? And how much influence and power should the public exert on public schooling? Should public be writ large, as some of the current critics recommend, that is, a national system of education? If we are to maintain the interests of the many publics, there can be no monolithic national system of education to serve certain vested interests. Who better knows the needs of the local public than those who live in the immediate community? Already too much of the curriculum is decided by the textbook publishing companies. This assumes, unfortunately, that too many teachers teach the textbook—that and nothing more. That is safe. Discussion of current issues—even though in the context of the course—can be dangerous. Classrooms are carefully monitored, and academic freedom is at risk in public schools. (I speak from personal experience.)

The critics assert that having many school districts is educationally unsound. The critics, of course, assume the districts would diverge from their predetermined curriculum and methodology. And only they have the wisdom and divine insight to know what is best for all.

An Aside

The most brilliant person I ever knew was my grandmother, who had all of two weeks of formal schooling and only with difficulty could write her name. The most effective school board member I ever knew—stereotyped as the old farmer—dozed while two college professors engaged in Gaston-Alphonse interchanges. When the vote was to be taken on an important issue, they took their cue from him—with his earthy common sense.

The common man who lives in the hinterland does not denigrate practical courses. To make a living is a high priority. There is a valuable place in the curriculum for distributive education, co-op education, and agricultural education. The critics need to know that this society needs competent auto repairmen, farmers, and factory workers and they make an essential contribution to the public at large . . . more than the versatile verbalizers.

The public schools must fit the needs of each particular community. Even adjacent school districts may differ greatly in curricula and methods. The public of the United States is diversified, and the public's children differ. The public's children need to know the meaning of citizenship (locally), geography (locally), history (locally), and mathematics (locally). The public's children need to learn in the context of local experiencing—not through abstractions of the distant and obscure. The public's children need more than learning through description; they need operational learning—both how to think as well as alternatives as to what to think.

A public school cannot be isolated from the community that it serves. There must be communication, not just information; there must be personal, meaningful involvement of the public. The public must be heard. How to do this? The Parent Teacher Organization is not enough. There needs to be lay involvement in committees concerned with school finance, building, and curriculum. These committees should be required to present their findings to the board of trustees. But these lay groups need to be part of committees that include teachers and administrators. The public needs to be educated about the reality of schooling (even visitation), and the teachers and administrators need to have feedback from the lay public. Yes, this will require extra time for busy people, but it is worthwhile, and this process can work to make the school even better. I have seen the harshest critic who served on a subcommittee of curriculum through dialogue and discussion become a public school advocate when he discovered the perceptions he had were incorrect. Those who have never been involved with the process will say it is idealistic. My experience says it can work with the proper dedication and intent of the public concern.

Lay people can be involved as paraprofessionals, guest "teachers." Senior citizens have much to offer young children.

Minority children, when there are no minority teachers, can find identification and role models through paraprofessionals.

Although the community school concept is rarely discussed these days, it has much to offer urban schools as well as rural schools—especially if it is thought of as an organic whole. Theodore J. Kowalski, writing in *Contemporary Education*, says: "Today, there are indicators of revival portending the possible second coming of community education."[1] But "for the concept to have a decent chance for success there must be a cadre of forward-thinking, risk taking administrators who are willing to learn new skills such as conflict management and group decision making. Additionally, some perennial questions must be answered satisfactorily to create a knowledge base for practitioners."[2]

Kowalski lists eight reasons for the renewed interest in community education.

1. A growing percentage of the citizenry no longer has contact with the public schools. Groups, such as senior citizens, often are reluctant to support a social agency they believe to be irrelevant to their personal needs. School administrators are seeking creative ways to regain this support of adults who do not have children enrolled in school.

2. American society is accepting the concept of lifelong education. Where education once was considered to be exclusively for children, society now accepts the notion that schooling may be needed or desired throughout one's life. Thus, there are increasing demands for the public schools to address needs of nontraditional students.

3. Social problems are a growing concern for educators. For example, the increasing number of one-parent families in American society has evolved as a major issue for many local school districts (and communities). Public schools are discovering that they cannot ignore these problems; yet correspondingly, the schools are declaring that they do not possess the human and physical resources necessary to address these social issues adequately.

4. Increases in leisure time prompt citizens to alter their life-styles and to expect more services from governmental agencies, for example, recreational programs. Many are looking to the schools (and their facilities) to provide some of these services. When their costly facilities stand empty a good portion of the time, the public schools become prime candidates to sponsor community services expansion.

5. The rapid distension of technology will require many citizens to undergo occupational retraining in their lives. The schools are a primary resource expected to contribute resources to meet these needs. The concept of lifelong learning encourages adult education for varying reasons, and economic factors connected to the labor force dictate vocational expansion in adult schooling.

6. The proliferation of research in fields such as organizational psychology and leadership studies produced a theory which suggests that public organizations can profit from conflict. Conflict now is viewed as inevitable, endemic, and often legitimate. Progressive school leaders are exhibiting a greater willingness to experiment with new decision-making processes based on this evidence. (Owens, 1981)

7. Although the public image of education appears to be rising, the recent concerns expressed in national studies and essays have had a profound impact upon the education profession. Educational administrators realize that merely perpetuating the status quo may be a practice unacceptable to the community. Public schools no longer enjoy the monopoly status that once allowed them to remain static and isolated from public scrutiny.

8. Declining birth rates created additional concerns for large numbers of school systems. Fewer students resulted in more unused space, and more unused space increased taxpayer concerns about cost efficiency. No doubt there are other reasons for the revival of interest in community education in addition to those presented here. This listing, however, includes the more cogent reasons why school administrators are once again seeking information about community education.[3]

The November 1972 special issue of *Phi Delta Kappan* dealt with community education. Several of the articles are worth rereading in the context of the 1980s. V. M. Kerensky's article, "Correcting Some Misconceptions about Community Education," lists six misconceptions. They are as follows: "a neat package of programs; an extended curriculum in late afternoon and evening for adult education and/or a few exciting activities; an expanded recreation program; a public relations gimmick; a delivery system—bringing education to more people; and several micro elements."[4] Kerensky believes that community educators seek a new form of education, a new philosophy, a macro concept. He writes that it "mobilizes heretofore untouched physical and human resources for educational, cultural growth."[5] It is a total community education process.

Without question this is a translation of the pragmatic philosophy of Dewey, Mead, and others (almost a century ago) to fit current educational problems. It was a good idea then; it is a good idea now. The school is *in* and *of* the community.

In 1939, Elsie Ripley Clapp wrote, *Community Schools in Action*. Her focus was on rural schools, just as the better known Flint, Michigan, community school experiment was urban in focus.

Note: In 1972, it was reported that there were twenty-five centers for community education at institutions of higher education across the country, providing consultant and supportive services to districts.

In 1971, there were 1,920 community schools.[6]

In the foreword to Clapp's book, John Dewey writes: "Perhaps the first lesson it [the book] teaches us is that schools function socially only when they function in a community for community purposes, and communities are local, present, and close by, while society at large is something vaguely in the distance."[7]

Be it noted that Clapp's book was an account of something actually done and how it was done. It was not theory—abstract or academic, it affected the life and well-being of the people of the community.

Dewey goes on to say:

> The neighborhood is the prime community; it certainly is so for the children and youth who are educated in the school, and it must be so for administrators and teachers if the idea of socially functioning schools is to take on flesh and blood. There is no occasion for fear that the local community will not provide roads leading out into wider human relations if the opportunities it furnishes are taken advantage of.[8]

Dewey paraphrases Lincoln's words: This is a school not only *for*, but *of* and *by* the community. Dewey points out that "teachers in the schools prepared themselves for their work by becoming citizen members of the community in the most intimate way."[9]

Teachers' relationships were face-to-face, and they involved themselves with the "process of educating themselves as to the community needs and resources, its weaknesses and strong points; they learned that only in this way could they engage in further education of the community. They did not survey the community; they belonged to it."[10]

Elsie Clapp's book, long forgotten by both educators and academicians, needs to be read in the context of what is happening in the decade of the 1980s. The ideas should not be copied as the Job Corps was à la the CCC—not taking cognizance of the changing social-cultural settings—but rather as a means of appropriating ideas to be reconstructed in today's schools. Fascinating items in Elsie Clapp's *Community School in Action* are the following: "Baby Clinics in 1936," "The Older People," "Starting a Nursery School in a Rural Community," and "Bringing the Community into the Work of the School."

And who today remembers Margaret Naumburg, founder of the Walden School in 1914 (a new type of educational experiment)? In 1928 in her introduction to *The Child and the World* she wrote:

> Through Francis Parker and John Dewey our schools were freed from the barren ideals of a monastic discipline. For the first time

they were brought close to the everyday life and genuine concerns of the children . . . but . . . since then . . . a curious distortion and modification [has occurred] in practice. . . . From being an attempt to orient children to the life of their own community, it has gradually been transformed into an effort to train children into a realization of their social responsibilities for citizenship. . . . It was not long before this ideal was transformed into extreme dogmas of an "Americanization program."[11]

Sound familiar? Words and verse may change, but the rhythm and rhyme remain. She was fearful that: "An exaggeration of the social ideal may lead to the extinction of individuality."[12]

And let us not forget Caroline Pratt and her Play School in Greenwich Village—in an intelligent, artistic setting. It too was a community school, even as a school of dramatics, play, and self-expression: As she wrote: "But the great value of dramatics to children of eleven, twelve, and thirteen lies in the positive working toward a common end. Individuals constantly stand aside for the benefit of the whole."[13]

And her message for the 1980s is clear: Schooling need not be pain, work, and worry: "We have always accepted it as natural for a child to play . . . but it is a fairly rare thing for adults to help enrich and extend this play. And it is quite a new theory to do this in schools."[14] Pratt saw early dramatic play as helping children in the future—in habits of searching for and using what lies about them. To her: "Pretend is the essence of drama. It marks quite a change in the growing up process."[15]

Some of the earlier concepts of community education seemed to ignore early childhood education (exceptions noted above). Perhaps the new conception of community education will include nursery schools, day-care centers within the school program, and even senior citizen centers.

Community education if flexible and fitted to local needs can give a new, positive definition of the neighborhood school. If community education is viewed as a product (to fit the current effective schooling thrust), it will become only another panacea that fails.

Public schools must also continue to follow-through on their graduates. The commencement exercise must not be a terminal celebration. The relationship between the student and the school must continue. Follow-up studies, and even more personal contact with students must continue. This can provide an overall evaluation of "how we are doing"—not just in terms of curriculum, but also of instruction and school climate.

A chilling incident happened just yesterday as I was writing this. A student dropped in to talk. (I put aside my pencil.) And when she left she said, "Thanks for talking with me." This speaks volumes for those truly interested in improving schooling. It is *a human* enterprise. There must be listening and communication!

References

1. Theodore J. Kowalski, "The Second Coming of Community Education," *Contemporary Education* 57, no. 4 (Summer, 1986), p. 194. Reprinted by permission of *Contemporary Education* and Theodore J. Kowalski, Dean, Teachers College, Ball State University, Muncie, Indiana.
2. Ibid., p. 197.
3. Ibid., pp. 27–30.
4. V. M. Kerensky, "Correcting Some Misconceptions About Community Education," *Phi Delta Kappan* 54, no. 3 (November 1972), pp. 158–59.
5. Ibid., p. 159.
6. Jack Minzey, "Community Education: An Amalgam of Many Views," *Phi Delta Kappan* 54, no. 3 (November 1972), p. 150.
7. John Dewey, Foreword in *Community Schools in Action*, by Elsie Ripley Clapp (New York: Viking Press, 1939), p. viii.
8. Ibid.
9. Ibid.
10. Ibid., pp. viii–ix.
11. Margaret Naumburg, *The Child and the World: Dialogue in Modern Education* (New York: Harcourt, Brace and Company, 1928), pp. xvii–xviii.
12. Ibid.
13. Caroline Pratt, "Growing Up and Dramatics," in *Creative Expression: The Development of Children in Art, Music, Literature, and Dramatics*, ed. Gertrude Hartman and Ann Shumaker (New York: John Day Company, 1932), p. 265.
14. Ibid., p. 262.
15. Ibid., p. 263.

PART III
THE REALITY

Chapter Seven

The Immoralists

The Principle of Circularity*

Aggression begets aggression; violence begets violence. In human relations, as well as in physics there is natural law: For every action there is a reaction.

In personal terms, when a person reacts—whether by brute force, by manipulation, or by legalisms, one morning the mirror will reflect that which he/she despises. Thoreau wrote that when a person is shocked at vice, he expresses a lingering sympathy with it: "We are double-edged blades, and every time we whet our virtue the return stroke straps our vice" (The Heart of Thoreau's Journals, p. 32).

When a reference group exerts excessive pressure on the body politic—implicitly or explicitly, the hidden agenda will eventually [come] out and become a lightening rod to pent up anger, frustration . . . and the reference group will reap the whirlwind.

What is true of individuals and reference groups is true of nation states. There was no American revolution. The frontier of colonial America was more democratic than the United States after the constitution: Women could vote in most colonies and Indians and blacks had rights and freedoms. After the constitution went into effect, the social-political setting regressed to a prior elitism

*Originally published in *Contemporary Education* 58, no. 3 (Spring, 1987), p. 125. Used by permission.

of land and wealth. Revolution simply replaces one ideology with another.
Michael Kort, author of The Soviet Collossus: A History of the USSR, writes:

> *But any revolution, no matter how drastic its ends or means, inevitably reflects the historical legacy of a nation's culture, customs, attitudes, and institutions (p. 7).*

On at least one matter this writer can agree with William J. Bennett. Recently public schools have ignored character education—primarily because too often the public cannot make the distinction between sectarian indoctrination and common decency. But prerequisite to moral literacy is the actual infusion into public education of respect for others, courtesy, honesty, and integrity. It can't be the cross-eyed bear complex (the cross I bear), that is, speaking or parroting dogma but not understanding. As Bennett himself wrote: "Good people—people of character and moral literacy—can be conservative, and good people can be liberal; good people can be religious, and good people can be non-religious."[1] As recent events have so dramatically illustrated, there is a difference between being religious and having a religion. Sometimes it appears that having a religion is incompatible with being religious. Being religious is a very personal matter.

In his first major address, William Bennett said that forming "character must begin in the home, starting in the earliest childhood years, but that afterwards school must help—because as President Eliot of Harvard once reminded us, in the campaign for character no auxiliaries are to be refused. And the school can be a mighty auxiliary."[2]

Time (May 25, 1987) had a cover article on "What Ever Happened to Ethics." Ethics is now the center of a new national debate.

To be ethical, to be moral is simply to follow the Golden Rule, that is, to be decent to others.

Decent is an old-fashioned word like integrity, loyalty, responsibility—words no longer in vogue. The hip words are greed, get yours, disinformation, and manipulation.

In schooling, the indecencies perpetuated against children and youth are a national disgrace. Children and youth are no longer persons, but products subject to the harassment of ideologues, bureaucrats, and politicians. Children and youth are the scapegoats to the ethical malaise that radiates from Wall Street, Congress, and the warrens within the Belt Way.

Specifically and explicitly, children and youth are treated indecently when teachers try to force them to learn before they are psychologically and physiologically ready. They are treated indecently when they are labeled, grouped, and stereotyped to expedite indoctrination in "right thinking." They are treated indecently when autonomy is violated by intolerable requirements that have nothing to do with life and living. They are treated indecently when test scores are substituted for evaluation and the teaching act is form without substance. They are treated indecently when schools have become concentration camps (Paul Goodman)—or relocation centers for remediation "in knowing their place" in a racist, elitist, and nihilistic society.

It must be noted that long before the evolution of public elementary and secondary schooling in this country, the central purpose of education was sectarian: it was indoctrination in the right dogma in order to delude the old Satan. Then, in the mid-nineteenth century, the common schools that proliferated under the guise of "an educated citizenry" were essentially Protestant schools. In the early sixties with a spate of Supreme Court decisions, Catholic students returned to the public schools, not only because of financial difficulty, but because public schools were becoming increasingly non-Protestant. Then began the mass exodus of conservative Christians to establish their own sectarian schools. Public schooling, it appears, is coming full circle with respect to character education, religion, and morality.

Public schooling is facing major moral questions, but tragically with the cult of efficiency and accountability pervading school systems and society, ethics is neglected or ignored. What follows is a modest list of the major moral dilemmas that must be faced by public educators. For want of a better designation, they are called *demonotrends.*

83

A. The average, the ordinary student, is neglected (and they are the majority student body), while attention and money are heaped on the special student. As noted by Phyllis McGinley in her poem "The Lament of the Normal Child," schools only "cherish the problem cases"[3]—or so it appears. This is nothing new.

In 1934, E. W. Butterfield was writing about the new 50 percent. He identified these students as those who could not meet the standards for admission and/or could not make satisfactory progress in the subjects of the secondary school curriculum. He saw an opportunity at that time to educate large groups for the actual life that they were living and were to live. They were to be educated for jobs—satisfying and monetarily rewarding. He was also writing about another 25 percent who would be trained for skilled trades and another 25 percent of the young people who would continue their education through professional specialization.[4]

In 1939, Charles A. Prosser recommended that all high-school students spend a minimum of 50 percent of their study on life-education subjects. These subjects would be the core of the curriculum, rather than college-preparatory courses. He believed this more democratic scheme would cater to the five who go directly to life, rather than to the one who goes directly to college. He did not see the life-education thrust as hurting the college-bound student.[5] Six years later at a meeting of the Vocational Education Division of the U.S. Office of Education, Prosser introduced a resolution calling for a program for the students in the educational no-man's land of the general track (60 percent of high-school youth), which would prepare them for satisfying lives and gainful employment. It was labeled *life-adjustment education*.[6] This was throwing down the gauntlet to the ever-present critics of public schooling.

As recently as 1971, Sidney P. Marland, then U.S. Commissioner of Education, criticized school administrators for being primarily concerned with college-entrance expectations while neglecting vocational-technical education. He noted that each year some 1.5 million youngsters either drop out of high school or end their formal schooling without any preparation for skilled occupations. He would adopt the term *career education* for vocational education.[7] *Career education* appears to have been a more happy designation than *life-adjustment*.

And what will not be discussed by the media, by the bureaucrats, and by the politicians is the changing public school population. Increasingly the public school student is coming from disadvantaged homes, from single-parent homes and all the while, the critics of public schooling are demanding more vigor, more academic courses—unrelated to the real world these children face now and tomorrow. What can be predicted? The dropout rate will accelerate. There must be transition from the artificial world of schooling to the real world of work—sooner or later. These skills of living in the real world must not be denigrated.

Harold L. Hodgkinson of the Institute for Educational Leadership, Inc., has summarized the education consequences of demographic changes as follows:

1. More children entering school from poverty households.
2. More children entering school from single-parent households.
3. More children from minority backgrounds.
4. A small percentage of children who have had Head Start and similar programs, even though more are eligible.
5. A larger number of children who were premature babies, leading to more learning difficulties in school.
6. More children whose parents were not married, now 12 of every 100 births.
7. More "latch-key" children and children from "blended" families as a result of remarriage of one original parent.
8. More children from teen-age mothers.
9. Fewer white, middle-class, suburban children, with day care (once the province of the poor) becoming a middle class norm as well, as more women enter the work force.
10. A continuing decline in the level of retention to high school graduation in virtually all states, except for minorities.
11. A continued drop in the number of minority high school graduates who apply for college.

12. A continued drop in the number of high school graduates, concentrated most heavily in the Northeast.
13. A continuing increase in the number of Black middle class students in the entire system.
14. Increased numbers of Asian-American students, but with more from Indonesia, and with increasing language difficulties.
15. Continuing high drop-outs among Hispanics, currently about 40% of whom complete high school.
16. A decline in the number of college graduates who pursue graduate studies in arts and sciences.
17. A major increase in part time college students, and a decline of about 1 million in full time students. (Of our 12 million students, only about 2 million are full time, in residence, and 18–22 years of age.)
18. A major increase in college students who need BOTH financial and academic assistance. A great liaison between the offices of student financial aid and counseling will be essential.
19. A continuing increase in the number of college graduates who will get a job which requires no college degree. (Currently 20% of all college graduates.)
20. Continued increases in graduate enrollments in business, increased undergraduate enrollments in arts and sciences COURSES but not majors.
21. Increasing numbers of talented minority youth choosing the military as their educational route, both due to cost and direct access to "high technology."
22. Major increases in adult and continuing education outside of college and university settings—by business, by government, by other non-profits such as United Way, and by for-profit "franchise" groups such as Bell and Howell Schools and The Learning Annex.
23. Increased percentage of workers with a college degree. (From one in seven to one in four today.)[8]

   B. Tracking and homogeneous grouping is immoral as well as educationally unsound. Not the least of the sins is the labeling of students—even at a very early age. William H. Whyte, Jr., puts it well: "Of all the forms of wanton self-destruction, the

Englishman A. A. Bowman once observed, there is none more pathetic than that which the human individual demands that in the vital relationships of life he be treated not as an individual but as a member of some organization."[9] (Substitute "group" for "organization" in the quote.)

Limited criteria are often used for grouping students, and students are often penalized simply because of their socioeconomic background, race, ethnicity, and even sex. Too often teachers assume that a homogeneous group is just that—and students are taught as a *group.*

Students are sophisticated as to the real meaning of course designations, such as basic mathematics, general science, and college English. If students are perceived by teachers and fellow students as underachievers (whatever that means) or overachievers (whatever that means), there is a tendency for them to perform to expectations. Methodology and technique are often deadly drill and repetition for lower-tracked students. Too frequently gifted and talented students simply get more, not different—in terms of content, methodology, and organization.

An additional reality in homogeneous grouping is that the novice teacher is given the "slower" classes while the more experienced teachers are given the "fast track" students. Similarly, in large school districts the beginning teacher is given challenging teaching assignments such as in concentrated poverty areas.

Be this as it may, a major ethical (even legal issue) is whether students in the lower tracks (groups) have an equal opportunity for discussion and interchange of ideas with the larger peer group and whether they have been denied the opportunity to learn higher order cognitive skills when they are isolated from the "cream of the crop." To segregate "intellectually" in a democratic society is just as immoral as to segregate on the basis of race. The concept of multipotentiality, a student gifted in one content field is gifted in all, has long been discredited by research as well as by common sense.

C. It is immoral to treat children and youth as sense mechanisms, as objects and things. Paul Goodman in *Compulsory Mis-*

87

education stated it thus: "It is said that our schools are geared to 'middle-class values,' but this is a false and misleading use of terms. The schools less and less represent *any* human values, but simply adjustment to a mechanical system."[10]

Increasingly a student is nothing more, on the face of it, than a test score, a grade, a social security number—a line in a computer printout. It is amazing how many teachers and administrators do not even know the names of their students, especially at the secondary and college level.

The schools are only a reflection of the larger society, a society obsessed with ends, particularly material ends. Perhaps nothing better represents current immorality than Columbus University offering a course on corporate raiding: the art of war. Can Murder, Inc., be far behind? Only a fool now believes in a "gentleman's agreement": A man's (woman's) word is of no great moment. A handshake means nothing and a kiss much less.

Since the expressive decade of the sixties—when the code words were "If it feels good, do it"—we have seen such demonstrations of man's inhumanity to man especially as it relates to the young and the vulnerable. Philip Wylie was premature with his reference to the generation of vipers.

Freedom has become license—freedom no longer entails responsibility. It is no contradiction in terms to speak of liberal fascists or humanistic fascists. There are no longer criminals in jails or prisons: They are freedom fighters. All laws, it appears, are unjust laws.

The new immorality can best be expressed as: Get yours but don't get caught. Morality is determined by the egocentric, egotistical self. Let not existential theory be the scapegoat for the new immorality. Those who profess the existential faith—on the face of it—are ignorant of the underlying assumptions of this philosophical thrust.

How prophetic my fraternal grandmother was, so many years ago! She said, "People just have kids, grease them, and turn them loose." With the increasing evidence that the American family is becoming dysfunctional, can school teachers become foster parents or the significant other? Parents must accept responsibility for parenting rather than using the schools as a dumping ground. Cruel words—but honest. A sentence in *Growing Up in River City* sums it up: "There is evidence that a stable, affectionate family can keep a boy out of delinquency even though he is a failure in school, grows up in a lower-class culture, and has a record and reputation of aggressive maladjustment in school."[11]

There are many reasons for the problems in parenting. No longer are children economically of value: Children are no longer producers; they are consumers. As reported in *U.S. News and World Report* (1975): "Some economists estimate the total cost of raising a child to maturity and paying for college expenses at around $326,000—including the lost wages of a working mother who leaves the labor force for 18 years."[12] That same article also cites a frightening study: "One family counselor cites a recent study showing that the average family spends only about 30 minutes each week in serious discussion of family problems and issues."[13] There is the old saw: Those who talk together stay together. Sometimes one wonders if America's pets receive more attention than do our children.

Writing in *Newsweek*, Jerome Kagan, Harvard psychologist, argues that the fundamental cause of parental anxiety is "a lack of consensus on values." "Parenting," says Kagan, "means implementing a series of decisions about socialization of your child—what you do when he cries, when he's aggressive, when he lies or when he doesn't do well in school." Fifty years ago, he says, such decisions were easier to make because Americans possessed a common agreement about what good parents should do. In contrast, Kagan asserts, "there is no consensus in America today as to what a child should be like when he is a young adult—or about how you get him there."[14] Today the American family can no longer be defined. It is a time of flux and experimentation. The nuclear family now is only an option, among many.

And how often a child is conceived in the hope it will save a troubled marriage. But Angus Campbell, whose pioneering study was reported in *U.S. News and World Report*, says:

The highest degree of satisfaction with life occurs among young married people with no children.
As children enter the scene, happiness generally goes down and stress goes up.
When children pass their sixth birthday, the marriage again becomes more satisfactory.
Finally, when children are over 7 years of age and start moving out on their own, contentment again increases for their parents . . .[15]

Perhaps with the increasing problems of children and youth—drug addiction, suicide, teenage pregnancy, crime—there is the possibility that all these problems are only symptoms of an even larger problem. The desperate need of children and youth to find belonging, identity, and caring in a society that seems to not give a damn for anyone but No. 1. A sad commentary of this lack of caring is the pregnant child who will say, "I want something to love." But a baby is not a thing, and a baby with only custodial care will die.

D. It is immoral to cheat children out of childhood. With the increasing pressure to push subjects further and further downward, on what has been called the educational ladder, little recognition has been given to the research on child growth and development, especially the concepts of brain growth "periodization" and "holistic readiness." It is criminal to try to force the children to learn material beyond their physical and mental capacity. Children can be "burnt out," suffering from stress, by the primary grades. A child is not a miniature adult, as many of our current critics would have us believe. No consideration is given to the fact that an individual child progresses at his or her own individual growth rate—physically, socially, emotionally, cognitively. No consideration is given to the fact that boys may be anywhere from six to eighteen months behind girls in their early years. No consideration is given to the fact that mental discipline and transfer of training (except for identical elements) are passé as psychological theories—unless one believes in the principles of learning practiced during the Middle Ages. Behaviorism may work well for pigeons and rats, but children are not animals. In childhood there must be time to play and exploration. Children must not be used by parents and others to achieve goals they themselves were never able to obtain.

In fact, I take this "push, push, push," "hurry, hurry, hurry" as a personal affront. I did not understand mathematics, even the basics, until on my own I read Charles Hubbard Judd as a graduate student. I studied mathematics in public schooling to get the right answer. The first summer after I got my doctorate, I enrolled at Macalaster College during the summer session to take Children's Literature and Art Appreciation. My college schedule did not allow me to take many courses I wanted to take.

It is necessary that we teach children subject matter, not teach subject matter to children. It is necessary that we help children develop their own cognitive structures—the halfway house, the vehicle for learning—rather than drilling them in facts, in knowledge. Only the individual child can organize, develop relationships—and because they want to learn, not because they have to learn.

E. It is immoral to be obsessed with minimum standards in education. A mental set has developed, a psychological climate, where "getting by" is enough, where schooling becomes a game. Schooling becomes periodic—step one, step two—a series of ends, jumping the schooling hurdles to get "the union card," that is, the Ph.D. degree. Even in the earliest grades, students are not interested in learning—"What do we have to learn this for?"—but all that matters is passing the test, getting the grade. It is not unusual for parents to give five dollars (minimum standard) for every A on the report card or to buy the high school graduate a new car. Minimum competency is achieved by explicit rewards.

A modest proposal is that consideration be given to the maximum rather than the minimum. The best teacher is the one who, rather than keeping students together page by page, encourages heterogeneity. The best teacher encourages students to proceed on their individual agendas—to explore, to be excited about their interests. But that's not in the rigid lesson plans of the ideologues, bureaucrats, or politicians. Public schools must not become "relocation centers" or centers of indoctrination in right thinking. Public schools are not places where children and youth are to be told what to think, but places where students learn how to think. Public schools need to give time for pondering, not rushing; for pleasure, not punishment; for issues, not propaganda. Public schools should not be isolation cells, that is, study carrels or classrooms, but should open windows and doors to the public.

References

1. William J. Bennett, "Moral Literacy and the Foundation of Character," *Daughters of the American Revolution Magazine*, February 1987, p. 94.
2. Ibid., p. 72.
3. *The New Yorker*, March 23, 1935.
4. E. W. Butterfield, "The New Fifty Per Cent," *Junior-Senior High School Clearing House*, January 1934.
5. Charles A. Prosser, *Secondary Education and Life* (Cambridge, Mass: Harvard University Press, 1945).
6. United States Office of Education, *Life Adjustment Education for Every Youth*, Bulletin no. 22, (Washington, D.C.: U.S. Government Printing Office, 1951), pp. 15–16.
7. Sidney P. Marland, Jr., "Career Education Now" in Keith Goldhammer and Robert E. Taylor (eds.), *Career Education*, (Columbus, OH: Merrill, 1972), p. 35.
8. Harold L. Hodgkinson, *All One System: The Demographics of Education Through Graduate School* (Washington, D.C.: Institute for Educational Leadership, 1985), p. 10. Reprinted by permission of the Institute for Educational Leadership.
9. William H. Whyte, Jr., *The Organization Man* (Garden City, N.Y.: Doubleday and Company, Inc., Doubleday Anchor Books, 1956), p. 66.
10. Paul Goodman, *Compulsory Mis-education* (New York: Horizon Press, 1964), p. 26.
11. Robert J. Havighurst, et al., *Growing Up in River City* (New York: John Wiley and Sons, Inc., 1962), p. 88.
12. "As Parents' Influence Fades—Who's Raising the Children?," *U.S. News and World Report*, October 27, 1975, p. 41.
13. Ibid.
14. Kenneth L. Woodward with Phyllis Malamud, "The Parent Gap," *Newsweek*, September 22, 1975, p. 48.
15. Angus Campbell, "Today's Marriages: Wrenching Experience or Key to Happiness," *U.S. News and World Report*, October 27, 1975, p. 35.

Chapter Eight

The Quantifiers

Caveats in Counting*

Has it come to this: That the human being is nothing more than a hole in a punch card or a social security number. Even the so-called helping professions have been caught in the quantitative trap: Whatever exists must be measured; whatever exists must be tested.

The only statistic one can truly count on is: $N = 1$. That truly human aspect of each of us cannot be measured, cannot be tested. As Thoreau wrote: "Perhaps the facts most astounding and most real are never communicated by man to man." To use expressions such as cohort, underclass, instrumental decade is only a cognitive arrow in flight, and each arrow has its own nomenclature.

The only datum that the social-psychological researcher has is a living, breathing human organism. To advocate, with subliminal hidden agenda, and to begin the discovery process by setting out to prove is to make machinery of poetry and to turn music to noise.

It was Banesh Hoffman who wrote in The Tyranny of Testing *(1962): A person who used statistics does not thereby automatically become a scientist any more than a person who uses a stethoscope automatically becomes a doctor. Nor is an activity necessarily scientific because statistics are used in it (p. 143).*

In counting, in measuring, quantifying, we are learning more and more about less and less—until one day we ask: What was the question after all? Was this worthwhile after all?

*Originally published in *Contemporary Education*, 56, no. 1 (Fall 1985). Used by permission.

Through the myth of objectivity—with all our measuring tools—we commit the most heinous of all crimes: We incarcerate, institutionalize our children into a world of simulation where they cannot be curious, play, or ask questions, or grow at their own pace.
There are no ones and twos in nature, and perhaps only children know that.

The major flaw in the so-called reform movement in American schooling is that the formulators, almost without exception, do not know the difference between quality and quantity. And there is a difference. Quality is illusive: Quality has to do with excellence and fineness—not easily framed by reason and knowledge. Like art, quality is not measurable. Quantity, in contrast, is easy to grasp: Quantity has to do with amount and degree. Quantity is easy to measure, easy to systemize, organize, and categorize. (I still remember the cartoon caption on the bulletin board behind my doctoral committee chairman's desk: "There must be a harder way.") Quality has something to do with listening, internalizing . . . quietness; quantity has something to do with rapid fire verbalization—doing, doing, doing—being accountable.

Colleagues often snicker when I recommend Robert M. Persig's *Zen and the Art of Motorcycle Maintenance* as must reading for those who would be educators. Persig's was a quest not for certainty, but for quality. He saw intellectuals as having the greatest difficulty *in seeing* quality: They must put everything in an intellectual straitjacket (my words, not his). And to him the ones who have the easiest time *in seeing* quality were small children, uneducated people, and culturally "deprived" people.[1] (My own experience with creative writing indicated that the troubled, special students were the ones with ideas and feelings, while the A students were letter perfect: Their work was form without substance. They conformed to the proper intellectual form.)

An analogy is appropriate: The reform movements today are much like the leaves and small twigs of trees (facts, mnemonics, information—just twirling in the wind). And how quickly the leaves fall with the first frost. In contrast, what is truly needed is a whole tree consisting of a bole and large branches reaching out to let the leaves take in the sunlight. The individual person needs to discover his/her individual boles (cognitive structures) and leaf it out with information and knowledge and see relationships—not only between content fields but to life experiences. A small, sturdy forest of a few acres is quality; acres and acres of saplings swaying with the slightest storm is quantity. There is the old saying: They can't see the tree for the forest. And it's also true that it's not what you look at, it's what you see.

Of course, in this day and age, there must be a scapegoat for all this quantification. Why not Horace Mann, perhaps our first *educational* researcher? It was he who determined the number of floggings administered during a school week and the minutes of recitation for each pupil during the school day. Basic research! Descriptive research still persists, and it has its place. But why not more action research in individual schools and districts—which can effect changes in curriculum and instruction? But never mind: That deals with the practical and the real. Today experimental research is in vogue—specific and esoteric—and the end result often is "no significant difference."

Another possible scapegoat for the obsession with quantification is Edward Lee Thorndike. He and his disciples provided the educational theorem: whatever exists, exists in some amount and can be measured. He and his disciples pontificated the laws of learning—effect, intensity, recency. And these laws of learning still live in the psychology of behaviorism, the psychology that undergirds most of the reform movements in education whose future is Walden II and George Orwell's 1984.

Robert Holmes Beck, writing in 1965, said: "Today, in the United States, professional students of education tend increasingly to work as scientists; in the future, this trend surely will not be reversed."[2] How right he was: the trend has accelerated.

But just exactly what does it mean "increasingly to work as scientists?" There is the scientific movement of step 1, step 2, step 3 . . . and the answer is. . . . There is the scientific movement of conjecturing consequences, generating hypotheses, and reaching tentative conclusions.

It was at the turn of the century that the great debate began as to what the scientific study of education really was. The debate was between the Herbartians and the Deweyans. And the present reform movements indicate that Dewey lost the debate. Today the scientific study of education is to set out to prove the predetermined conclusions—it is not to discover; it is to uncover. Now we have Karl Pearson's mathematical constructs, now we have James McKeen Cattell's mental tests and measurements, and now we have Alfred Binet's and Lewis Terman's tests of intelligence, and now we have Cliff Stone's and Edward Thorndike's objective tests and scales. We now have the sophisticated tools and devices to quantify and quantify, to measure and to measure . . . and when all is said and done, what is the measure of a man? Is it possible that what is truly important about a human being cannot be measured and quantified? Can we measure the quality of a person's life? Creativity? Empathy? (To me, the greatest person who ever lived was my maternal grandmother—unschooled, unlettered, but she had the quality of a shining star . . . to me, to family, to community. She lives in the spirit, not as a dry name on a printed page.)

Educators need to know that the scientific study of education is supplementary to the art of teaching. To say a method or procedure *works* is not enough. *Works* in terms of what? In what context? In terms of long-term consequences? Descriptively and operationally? From what perspective? From what particular philosophical/sociological/psychological bias?

The heart of the scientific study of education as applied to the individual classroom comes down to this: Lesson plans. Are the plans described with the specific behavioral objectives and explicit performance outcomes? Or are the plans more flexible—something in the mode of Ralph Tyler and Hilda Taba?

The focus on lesson plans is not in the broad terms of curriculum development, but as one day in the life of an individual classroom—as a part of a continuing, related process. Daniel Tanner and Laurel N. Tanner translate Tyler's questions as follows: "In essence, Tyler's questions represent the four-step sequence of (1) identifying objectives, (2) selecting the means for the attainment of these objectives, (3) organizing these means, and (4) evaluating the outcomes."[3]

Perhaps a better term than *lesson plans* is *lesson planning*. This is time for digression, for capitalizing on current events. (My own personal experience tells me this: If I plan too well, too carefully, the lesson does not go well. If I plan too loosely, the lesson does not go well. I keep striving for the middle ground. As times goes by, I'm learning more about what that middle ground is *for me*.)

Those who believe that Dewey's criticism of Herbart's methodology, that is, his five steps, was a coup de grace to Herbart's teacher-content dominated style are misinformed. Herbart's five steps of preparation, presentation, association, generalization, and application are still practiced in many classrooms yet today—especially in mathematics and English. One day is like every other with its homework, a recapitulation, a little new material, reinforcement, assignment, and drill.

The quantifiers believe more is better. But a longer school year and a longer school day with more subjects is not necessarily better. Has any consideration been given to attention span? Change of pace? Intrinsic motivation? Consolidation for learning? Horizontal and vertical articulation? (A case in point: Assume an English teacher returns to summer school to take a course in the American novel and is required to read twenty-five novels in a five-week period, with the accompanying term paper and exams. Will the teacher be more turned on to reading novels, or will he never read another? Frankly, I'm shocked to discover how few English teachers continue to read— any-thing . . . novels, nonfiction, even magazines. To read one novel in depth and with appreciation is a quality experience; to read twenty-five novels, in fear and trembling, is quantity.)

The quantifiers believe in testing—the more the better. (Please note: Testing is not evaluation.) Most of the testing is so-called objective testing. (How many graduate students have told me, "This is the first essay exam I've had in my college career?") The most important elements of an education simply cannot be evaluated by an objective exam. Paradoxically, an objective exam is subjective in several ways, the selection of items, sophistication in selecting stems, usage and grammar in construction of items, standards established for passing, failing, or grading, the bias of the test maker . . . .

And, oh yes, what happens to the test results? Are they simply recorded, filed? If they are perchance used in parent-teacher conferences, has the guidance counselor held in-service meetings to help teachers report to parents in a responsible way? What about confidentiality? Are tests used to find weaknesses in the curriculum—or a technique used by the current reform-movement posse to evaluate teachers? What is truly frightening is that teachers caught in the catch-22 trap of trying to educate students or train them to pass tests will obviously choose to drill students to pass exams, a game known as trivial pursuit.

The quantifiers judge a school not on the basis primarily of its "humanness"—the reformers see all public school students as being distressed, disadvantaged, and doomed to mediocrity. The quantifiers judge a school on the basis of heredity and pedigree—how old the ivy is, the "halo" effect. The quantifiers judge the whatness: How many computers? How "modern" the facilities—especially the scientific laboratories? And remember it was St. Conant in 1959 who recommended: "A school should have the *equipment* [italics added] for a developmental reading program."[4] That's how one improves reading! And it was Conant who recommended that: "In addition to the diploma, each student should be given a *durable record* [italics added] of the courses studied in four years and the grades obtained . . . . The record might be *cards* [italics added] that could be carried in a wallet."[5] In other words, schooling is a thing, summarized on a card. The quantifiers judge the school by buildings and grounds. (A personal reference: I never will forget the graduate student who said to me in the parking lot, pointing to a tree nearby, "That tree gets more respect around here than I do.")

In a sense, James Conant was the godfather of *A Nation at Risk* and of the quantifiers when he asserted ". . . that a high school must have a graduating class of at least one hundred to function adequately as a comprehensive school."[6] But little thought was given to the possibility that a school could become too large—even with schools within schools. And compare Conant's curricular recommendations for the academically talented

(p. 57) with the *minimum* requirements for all students (p. 24) in *A Nation at Risk: The Imperative for Educational Reform*. The difference is narrowing between the curricula required for academically talented students and that for all students.

The quantifiers can usually be identified by "double speak." They would support a nongraded system in the elementary school—which is really more graded and more systematic with its phases than the "old" graded system. The quantifiers would support flexible scheduling, which is less flexible than the old "one track schedule." Instead of the "old-fashioned" fifty-five minute periods, there would be modules, "mods," of fifteen to twenty minutes; then more subjects could be taught—that is, English and history could be taught in two "mods" for forty minutes rather than fifty-five minutes. Larger schools might have as many as seven or eight different schedules: French might be the first hour on one schedule, fourth hour on another. Students need a libretto for musical chairs. The quantifiers prefer semester courses—more is better. The quantifiers like prerequisites for advanced courses, a surreptitious way of expanding the racecourse.

Now the latest fad of the quantifiers is "time on task"—earlier known as time-and-motion studies. Quantifiers would be especially interested in innovative (double-speak) practices that would concentrate on materials that would be teacher proof . . . such as learning packets, programmed texts, teaching by television, workbooks, teacher manuals (which accompany reading texts), language laboratories, learning kits, et cetera, et cetera.

(A hypothetical situation: You are confronted with two major problems when you arrive at school in the morning. First, an elementary school child has been assaulted on the way home from school the previous afternoon, and second, obscene words have been painted in red on school sidewalks and buildings. Which problem would take first priority? I predict the paint problem would have higher priority than the personal problem.)

The quantifiers ask the question *what* is a person, not who is a person. (The bane of a student's existence is anecdotal records . . . the rap sheet. We were carefully taught in teacher training always to go through students' records before we met the class. I never did. I believed a child needed a new beginning with me—up front and in person.) What are the student's IQ scores? What are the student's grades? Is he/she a discipline problem? What is the socioeconomic background of the family? Does the student dress well, and is he or she clean—and not smell! (A delegation of teachers once came to me demanding that I do something about a teacher's body odor.)

Little by little in public schools, as well as in the larger society, individual freedoms are being nibbled away. Once I believed the romantic idealists or compassionate critics (Jonathan Kozol and John Holt, among others) were overstating the case, but now I truly wonder. Sit up straight. . . . Stop slouching. . . . Are you paying attention?. . . . Where's your homework? . . . This is the last time I tell you. . . . Do you want to go to the Dean? . . . You didn't read the assignment, did you? . . . What do you want a pass for this time? . . . Stop talking. . . . Line up, we're going to the bathroom. . . . Sharpen your pencil before the bell rings. . . . So you are tardy again. . . . I want the paper folded and your name in the upper right hand corner. . . .

The quantifiers would like to see schools operate like factories and produce a good product. The time is not too far distant when teachers and students will punch the time clock just like in a factory. Schools will be an assembly line, where each facet of the product will be measured for quality control. Teachers will be rewarded with plaques and money (merit pay) as to how well their products do. Now students are only branded with different kinds of diplomas. Perhaps the future will see students literally branded on graduation with different colored stars on their hands—or if not that, to be required to wear at all times, a badge of merit or demerit, to be truly accountable to the system.

References

1. Robert M. Persig, *Zen and the Art of Motorcycle Maintenance: An Inquiry Into Values* (New York: William Morrow and Company, Inc., 1974), p. 247.

2. Robert Holmes Beck, *A Social History of Education,* Foundations of Education Series (Englewood Cliffs, N.J.: Prentice-Hall, Inc., 1965), p. 95.
3. Daniel Tanner and Laurel N. Tanner, *Curriculum Development* 2d ed. (New York: Macmillan Publishing Co., 1975), p. 84.
4. James B. Conant, *The American High School Today: A First Report to Interested Citizens* (New York: McGraw-Hill Book Company, Inc., 1959), p. 67.
5. Ibid., p. 50.
6. Ibid., p. 14.

Chapter Nine

The Progressives

The Cycles of American Schooling*

I

Arthur M. Schlesinger, Jr., in The Cycles of American History *(1986) outlines alternative interpretations of the cyclical thesis, from the larger perspective of the domestic affairs of the nation-state. Public schooling, reflective of the large social configuration, also undergoes cyclic changes.*

Whether one defines these cyclic changes as shifts in national involvement between public purpose and private interest, between democracy and capitalism (Arthur Schlesinger, Jr.), a pendulumlike swing between the centralization and diffusion of national energy (Henry Adams), or each generation as a new people (Alexis de Tocqueville), the question that Arthur Schlesinger, Jr., poses is: "Why does the cycle move as it does?"

II

An alternative hypothesis to Arthur Schlesinger, Jr.'s thesis is that the quest for certainty is between two opposing ideologies embedded in the American psyche. The conflicting ideologies of the American dream were and are Idealism

*Originally published in Contemporary Education 58, no. 4 (Summer 1987), p. 185. Used by permission.

and Empiricism—one with roots in Germany, the other with roots in England. Contrary to Schlesinger's stance, there can be liberal as well as conservative ideologies. And this causes the cycles, the dialectics in policy and practice.

III

Arthur Schlesinger, Jr., points to an alternative to the cyclic when he refers to the distinctive American philosophy of William James, that is, pragmatic philosophy. Pragmatic philosophy is against ideology. It is a philosophy that strives for authentic dynamic concensus—of dialogue, discussion, openness. Pragmatic philosophy sees democracy as experiment, a growing, developing political organism rather than a panacea, a utopia.

So, in the context of a cyclic expression in American schooling, we need not be entrapped in the either/or proposition: Both the child and society are important, both heredity and environment are important, both process and product are important, both the affective domain and the cognitive domain are important, and both knowledge and intelligence are important.

IV

Today the emphasis is on societal needs, heredity, product, the cognitive domain, and knowledge. This is an instrumental ideology of testing, account-ability, and management reacting to the prior expressive ideology of humanness, alternative schooling, and self-discovery. Will the next cycle be a return to the expressive ideology?

Progress is a word colored by the ends in view. Progress is not just change—especially change for the sake of change. Progress can only be defined in the frame of one's own philosophical bias: the assumptions (or assertions) one makes about the basic questions of truth, reality, the good, the beautiful. . . . What is the relationship between the purpose and the goals? What are the means? Are the ends static or dynamic?

The abrasive denunciators of public schooling should be asked a few straightforward questions: Progress toward what ends? (These new ideologues are certainly not neutral or benign; they froth with fervor.) Do you, dear critic (reformer?), really believe in democratic schooling (education) for all the people's children? Or do you believe in a superior education for the chosen few—and training and/or indoctrination for the masses? In your diatribes against public schooling, do you believe in schooling (education) for the modern age or regressing to the philosophy, psychology, sociology of the Middle Ages? Is there implicit prejudice against Blacks, Hispanics, Native Americans—against the underclass, working class students—in your recommendations? It appears that only foreign Americans have access to television, to newspapers, to book publishers—to propagate their anti-American, anti-public schooling stance. An indigenous American system of public schooling has never been allowed to evolve. Yet the critics criticize what never was in reality—what existed only in theory—but the critics even insist on misinterpreting that theory—quoting one another in a campaign of disinformation.

Progress to the current crop of critics is moving backward to twenty-five, fifty, or a hundred years ago—another time, another place. It is déjà vu. The cycle keeps occurring, reoccurring. Progress from the democratic perspective is one step forward, two steps back—and the dialectics, the pendulumlike swing, seems to be accelerating.

George Santayana's famous quote—"Those who cannot remember the past are condemned to repeat it" (*The Life of Reason*, vol. 1)—has a flaw. According to a *U.S. News and World Report* article written in 1980:

> If you assume that 10 is the age at which an event creates a lasting impression on a person's memory, then . . .
> 85 percent do not remember the stock market crash.
> 74 percent are unable to remember the Great Depression.
> 68 percent cannot recollect World War II.
> 32 percent are too young to remember when man first landed on the moon.[1]

So when remembrance of things past is so limited, perhaps

every generation is doomed by its short history to repeat, in some degree, the mistakes of the past.

It was Thoreau who wrote: "A man is wise with the wisdom of his time only, and ignorant with its ignorance. Observe how the greatest minds yield in some degree to the superstitions of their age."[2]

In 1962, Earl C. Kelley wrote a wonderful little book called *In Defense of Youth.* "The attacks on education have been among adults all right, but they have caused teachers to become more rejecting of youth rather than more accepting."[3]

Those words were written some twenty-five years ago. They are even more appropriate today.

Kelley notes that:

> A list of the attackers could be pages long, but if it were, it would not contain the name of a single person who has made a study of teaching and learning. I suspect that this is the only area in the whole human knowledge where it seems to be granted that those who have not studied the problem, who are unfamiliar with the available research data, are generally accepted as knowing more about it than those who have.[4]

That hasn't changed in some twenty years. The attackers of the 1980s are glib gluttons of disinformation; by devious and manipulative means they are out to destroy public schooling in this country, so that their own private and parochial schools can prosper.

Kelley dared to speak out in the 1960s, but today even at the university level professors are at risk to tell the truth. There are student plants in classrooms who represent both the right and left ideologues. They differ only in technique: the ideologues of the left use anonymous phone calls, letters, stalking horses, indirect methods; the ideologues of the right use up-front, very direct methods.

Kelley wrote that the attackers have abandoned democracy: "They have repudiated the dream of America which holds that each individual is worthy, has value to the rest of us, and has a right to opportunity to achieve the maximum within his capacity. They have advocated the creation of a worthy and a worthless class establishing an intellectual elite bringing into being a class of the educationally disinherited."[5]

This drive by the attackers is even worse than twenty-five years ago. They use such devices as tuition tax credits, homogeneous grouping, and magnet schools—and propose such devices as the voucher system, performance contracting, and entrepreneurial schools: "They have demanded a return to the educational methods of the old world, in the face of the fact that most Americans or their ancestors fled the old world to escape offensive and inhuman ideologies best represented by their schools."[6]

Today most of the attackers consider the American public ignorant and noncaring, but there is increasing concern in the hinterlands about the American foreigners, who give their allegiance to another country. By using the media, television especially, the attackers are able, as Kelley wrote in 1962: "[By casting] doubt in the public mind as to the values of universal education, they have made it difficult to finance public education."[7]

And in 1962 Banesh Hoffman wrote *The Tyranny of Testing*. He wrote: "Tests are misused when they are taken too seriously. Though testing is no game, people in positions of responsibility would do well to treat it as one. Otherwise professional judgment becomes overawed and atrophied, and professional testers take over."[8]

Alas, this was written twenty-five years ago: Progress? Déjà vu? Testing, testing, testing is the password to the effective school movement.

Hoffman also wrote: "There is a place for multiple-choice tests, but it is a strictly limited one, and its bounds have long since been overstepped . . . except for the most superficial aspects of testing, multiple-choice tests are inherently defective no matter how well they are drafted."[9]

And it was twenty-five years ago that not only Conant established his twenty-one commandments for public schooling, but Lloyd J. Trump was in his heyday—with team teaching, programmed instruction, and teaching by television. Writing about the future in *Guide to Better Schools: Focus on Change*, Trump and Baynham said: "Instructional films and tapes will originate from a central studio and full cable installations will channel television and other audio facilities into school rooms where needed . . . automated and other programmed instruction devices will be standard equipment in laboratories and available for use in student cubicles and other independent study areas."[10]

There were other educational futurists who believed that libraries would no longer contain books—only video-audio tapes, microfilms, disc recordings. One might well ask where have all the language laboratories and programmed machinery gone? One might well ask what has happened to team teaching in the mode of Trump? Where are the schools where no bells ring?

Twenty-five years ago, the major thrust in public schooling was mechanistic and realistic under the leadership of the Conants and Trumps, yet there was a *countervailing* body of opinion as represented by educators such as Earl Kelley. While the educators' voices were rarely heard, the power elite propagated the ideas of those with the right ideology.

So it was some fifty years ago as well. Those who knew most about public schooling were little noted; those with the right credentials were given *access* to the press and pulpit.

Fifty years ago, amid the Great Depression, the fallout from the "Science of Education" period was still evident. It was Robert Holmes Beck who wrote: "Between 1900 and 1915, the scientific study in the United States matured . . . Between 1915 and 1935, testing and measuring in education were tremendously productive and useful."[11]

Beck then cites Bernie Smith's article "Science of Education" in the *Encyclopedia of Educational Research* to support his hypothesis: "In this period [1900–15] were developed statistical formulas, achievement tests, intelligence tests, and techniques of experimental control. . . . In addition, these instruments, techniques, and procedures were employed in evaluating the effectiveness of educational programs of organized research."[12]

Just as the honest reason for the development of the middle school concept was demographic and economic (and its justification developed ex post facto), so the prevailing reason for the success of William Wirt's "platoon system" (Gary, Indiana) had to do with economics and with the best use of facilities. The platoon system was the pop innovation of its day. The plan was hastily adopted by many school boards after little or no investigation.[13] Present-day reformers would be pleased to know that in the Gary Plan each of the standard subjects was categorized for rapid, normal, or slow learners and on the basis of tests and interviews each youngster was assigned an individual program. Learning was departmentalized and compartmentalized. There were even voluntary Saturday coaching sessions in each of the major fields. And, alas, the schools were to remain open all day, twelve months a year. In theory, the Gary Plan had some Deweyan aspects, such as community involvement, but that was theory. Theory and practice always seem to diverge. It almost seems that it is standard operating procedure for truly creative, innovative formulations to be prostituted in practice for economic or political reasons and profession of belief and practice to become contradictory.

But who perhaps best represents the practice of fifty years ago was Franklin Bobbitt. Bobbitt would apply the principles of "scientific management" used in the factory, in business, to education. He believed it was "possible to set up definite standards for the various educational products."[14] These products included administrators as well. Even today, what school district does not have explicit job descriptions for all its functionaries? Much like today, industry and business through the politicians they have bought and paid for would tell schools what to teach and how to teach it. For example, public school educators did not implement programmed machines or computers; they were forced on schools through manipulation and implicit pressure. There were no pilot projects. Rather, there were massive implementations. And under the guise of applying the techniques of business and industry to schooling, there was "performance contracting" in the 1960s—a glorious failure, one of the great coverups in educational research.

Not satisfied with applying his principles of the business-industrial complex to administration and the assembly line, Bobbitt turned next to curriculum. Here he would apply the principles of "educational engineering." He would survey the needs of the adult community and translate them to provide the structure and content of the curriculum. He wrote in 1924: ". . . discover what the activities are which make up a man's life and we have the objectives of education."[15]

This smacks of the long-enduring, traditional belief that schooling is periodic and terminal. But in addition, Bobbitt would have the adult experiences broken down into smaller and smaller units of study, with specific tasks to be performed. How similar to behavioral objectives of today in providing the units of study. How similar to Barak Rosenshine's "direct instruction" (1976)—with small steps and work mediated by teacher or workbook—or Benjamin S. Bloom's "mastery learning" (1976)—with the focus on smaller units. Both Bloom and Rosenshine are particularly attending to what may be labeled as "low-status" students in the public schools. So the more schooling seems to change, the more it stays the same.

It is appropriate to refer to Raymond E. Callahan's classic, *Education and the Cult of Efficiency*. In 1962, he wrote: "Doubtless many educators who had devoted years of study and thought to the aims and purposes of education were surprised to learn that they had misunderstood their function. They were to be mechanics, not philosophers."[16] What was true in 1962 is true today; what was true twenty-five years ago was true fifty years ago and one hundred years ago.

Go back one hundred years. William Graham Sumner, who Lawrence Cremin says was "the commanding figure of the new field of sociology,"[17] held the professorship of political and social science at Yale from 1872 until his death in 1910. As noted by Cremin, "his wholehearted espousal of social Darwinism undoubtedly did much to enhance the status of that creed both within and without the community of scholars."[18]

Sumner was no democrat. He saw progress "as winning more social power."[19] From the "increase of industrial power there follows advance in science, fine arts, literature, and education."[20] Power and progress came about in the competitive marketplace.

Like the current attackers of public schooling, Sumner did

not believe in equality. Unlike them, however, he was blunt. In his essay "Equality" he said: "The assertion that all men are equal is perhaps the purest falsehood in dogma that was ever put into human language."[21]

To his credit, Sumner noted the difference between schooling and education. His social-political orientation is clear. He believed it was unfortunate that people were pinning their faith on schooling. And he thought that faith in book-learning was one of the superstitions of the nineteenth century.[22] In his essay "Earth Hunger or the Philosophy of Land Grabbing," he actually stated that democracy itself was the pet superstition of the age.[23] He saw each man as having plenty of the rights of man simply by *being;* he does not need higher training and education to be valuable member of society.[24]

Sumner saw sensationalism and mischief in the common school as well as in the universities,[25] and he saw this mischief and sensationalism as applying to methods as well as to subjects.[26] The culprits, even then were "educators," men without education—men he saw as playing a pitiful role. But he saw education as labor, as developing mental power and discipline—and nothing to do with theorizing.[27]

The more the larger society changes, the more the critics stay the same. Not even the means have changed: The attackers still have the podium and the pulpit. And today those who know most about public schooling suffer the same benign neglect that Lester Frank Ward, William Graham Sumner's contemporary, suffered. Ward was egalitarian, believing in universal schooling. Ward was, even then, a symbol of the indigenous, quiet American schooling revolution—striving to emerge.

The ideas of Lester Frank Ward were diametrically opposed to the ideas of William Graham Sumner in almost every aspect of sociology and pedagogy—especially as to the nature of progress and purpose in education. In 1883, Lester Ward's two-volume work *Dynamic Sociology* was published—even before Albion Small became the head of the first department of sociology in the United States (Chicago, 1892). While Sumner was known by the layman, Ward was even unknown by most academicians.

In his introduction to *Lester Ward and the Welfare State*, Henry Steele Commager writes that in "the realm of social economy he anticipated Thorstein Veblen, in the realm of education he anticipated John Dewey" and "in the realm of politics he provided the intellectual foundations on which such men as La Follette and Wilson and Franklin Roosevelt were later to build."[28] Commager also wrote that he was "the first sociologist to challenge the doctrine of laissez faire on scientific grounds" and "the first to embrace the full implications of pragmatism and to give sociology a scientific foundation."[29] But it seems today the idealogues, the bureaucrats, and the politicians would have us return to laissez faire in schooling along the principles of William Graham Sumner.

To Lester Ward, "no progress is real that does not constantly show a reduction of the aggregate suffering or an increase of the aggregate enjoyment throughout society."[30] Unlike Sumner, Ward was a democrat, believing in equal opportunity, especially in education. In *Applied Sociology* he wrote that "every member of society is equally heir to the entire social heritage."[31] The task "is nothing less than the diffusion of all knowledge among all men."[32] Ward's *Applied Sociology* was published in 1906, but his words are alive today (as criticism) to all the legislation such as the National Defense Act and the Elementary and Secondary Act, to all the books such as *A Nation at Risk* and *The Paidea Proposal*, and to all the tirades against public schooling. He wrote: "The equalization of opportunity means the equalization of intelligence, and not until this is attained is there any virtue or any hope in schemes for the equalization of the material resources of society."[33] Even then, he knew his proposition that the lower classes of society are the intellectual equals of the upper class would probably shock most minds.[34] His point: the difference was (is) the difference in knowledge.[35] Today, E. D. Hirsch and Allan Bloom equate knowledge and intelligence. Too many of the knowledgeable today, as then, are without common sense, without intelligence—and are ignorant of that which they criticize.

Ward condemned private schools, but not generally as to

motives: "Except where they are instituted for sectarian propagandism, or to influence public opinion in the defense of vested interests, they usually emanate from motives as disinterested as any—often very high and bordering on the humanitarian.[36] Perhaps in the decade of the 1980s, the motives of the founders of the new Christian schools and certain private schools might be questioned. Are they simply the practical vehicles of the ideologues of the right and left? To Ward: "Education is really needed for the purpose of making better citizens."[37] He was quite clear that state education was better for the pupil and immeasurably better for society.[38]

Perhaps the greatest flaw in all the recommendations for the improvement of public schooling is the neglect of the affective domain. Children are not treated as holistic human beings; they are mechanisms to be measured. One of Ward's most poignant passages comes from *Dynamic Sociology:* "It is a mistake to suppose that the sole element of excellence is superior intellectual power. It is usually an average intellect joined to an indomitable will, a tenacious perseverance, or an unquenchable ambition. It is *emotional* force, not intellectual, that brings out exceptional results."[39]

So then as now, those who supported the evolution of an indigenous system of American schooling based on democratic principles were little noted. In fact, there appears to be a conspiracy of silence yet today by the power elite against those who support, through public schooling, the democratic ideal.

References

1. "When Voters Recall Less and Less," *U.S. News and World Report,* January 14, 1980, p. 56–57.
2. Odell Shepard (ed.), *The Heart of Thoreau's Journals* (Cambridge, Mass.: Houghton Mifflin Company, 1927), p. 160.
3. Earl C. Kelley, *In Defense of Youth* (Englewood Cliffs, N.J.: Prentice-Hall, Inc., 1962), p. 94.
4. Ibid.
5. Ibid., pp. 96–97.
6. Ibid., p. 97.

7. Ibid., p. 97.
8. Banesh Hoffman, *The Tyranny of Testing* (New York: Collier Press, 1962), p. 103.
9. Ibid., p. 216.
10. Lloyd J. Trump and Dorsey Baynham, *Guide to Better Schools: Focus on Change* (Chicago: Rand McNally and Co., 1961), p. 12.
11. Robert Holmes Beck, *A Social History of Education*, Foundation of Education Series (Englewood Cliffs, N.J.: Prentice-Hall, Inc.), p. 104.
12. Ibid.
13. Charles L. Spain, *The Platoon School* and Roscoe David Case, *The Platoon School in America* as cited in Laurence A. Cremin's *The Transformation of the School: Progressivism in American Education* (New York: Vintage Books, A Division of Random House, 1964), pp. 155–56.
14. Franklin Bobbitt, *The Supervision of City Schools: Some General Principles of Management Applied to the Problems of City-School Systems*, Twelfth Yearbook of the National Society for the Study of Education, part 1 (Bloomington, Ill., 1913), p. 11.
15. Franklin Bobbitt, "The New Technique of Curriculum Making," *Elementary School Journal* 25, September 1924, p. 49.
16. Raymond E. Callahan, *Education and the Cult of Efficiency* (Chicago: University of Chicago Press, 1962), p. 84.
17. Lawrence A. Cremin, *The Transition of the School: Progressivism in American Education, 1876–1956* (New York: Vintage Books, A Division of Random House, 1964), p. 94.
18. Ibid.
19. William Graham Sumner, "Power and Progress," in *The Challenge of Facts and Other Essays*, ed. Albert Galloway Keller (New Haven: Yale University Press, 1914), p. 147.
20. Ibid., p. 148.
21. William Graham Sumner, "Equality," in *Earth Hunger and Other Essays*, ed. Albert Galloway Keller (New Haven: Yale University Press, 1913), p. 88.
22. William Graham Sumner, "The Teacher's Unconscious Success" in *Earth Hunger*, essays, ed. Albert Galloway Keller (New Haven: Yale University Press, 1913), pp. 9–10.
23. William Graham Sumner, "Earth Hunger on the Philosophy of Land Grabbing," in *Earth Hunger*, p. 42.
24. Ibid., p. 45.
25. William Graham Sumner, "Integrity in Education," *Essays of William Graham Sumner*, ed. Albert Galloway Keller and Maurice R. Davie, vol. 1 (New Haven: Yale University Press, 1933), p. 37.
26. Ibid.
27. Ibid.
28. Henry Steele Commager, *Lester Ward and the Welfare State* (Indianapolis: Bobbs-Merrill Company, Inc., 1967), pp. xxvii–xxviii.
29. Ibid., p. xxxvii.
30. Lester M. Ward, *Dynamic Sociology or Applied Social Science as Based Upon Sociology and the Less Complex Sciences*, vol. 1 (1883; reprint, New York: D. Appleton Company, 1926), p. 67.
31. Lester M. Ward, *Applied Sociology: A Treatise on the Conscious Improvement of*

Society by Society (Boston: Ginn and Company, 1906), p. 307.
32. Ibid.
33. Ibid., p. 281.
34. Ibid., p. 97.
35. Ibid.
36. Ibid., p. 309.
37. Lester M. Ward, *Dynamic Sociology*, vol. 2, p. 589.
38. Ibid., pp. 590–591.
39. Ibid., p. 598.

Bibliography

1981

Hamm, Russell. *Philosophy and Education: Alternatives in Theory and Practice.* 2d ed. Danville, Ill.: Interstate Printers and Publishers, Inc., 1981.
————. "The Future of Middle School Education—the Decade Ahead." *Junior High–Middle School Bulletin* 19, no. 3 (Spring 1981).
Hamm, Russell L., and James E. Higgins. *A Study of the Curriculum and Testing Program in the Bango Community Schools.* Terre Haute: Bureau of School Services, School of Education, Indiana State University, 1981.

1980

Baker, Catherine A., and Russell L. Hamm. *The American Indian: A Teaching-Learning Unit,* Studies in Curriculum Development, no. 4. Terre Haute: School of Education, Indiana State University, 1980.
Hamm, Russell L. Editorial. *Contemporary Education* 51, Winter 1980.
————. "Meandering." *Contemporary Education* 51, Winter 1980.
Hamm, Russell L. and Kenneth T. Henson. "Philosophy: Curriculum Source and Guide." *Contemporary Education* 51 (Spring 1980).

1979

Hamm, Russell L. Poem. *Indiana Rural News,* August 29, 1979.

———. "Toward an Existential Methodology in the Language Arts." *Journal of Children and Youth* 1 (Fall 1979), pp. 15–17.

———. "Poetry: Rhythm, Rhyme, and Reason." In *Rhythm, Rhyme, and Reason,* proceedings of the 1979 Ninth Annual Reading Conference, ed. David C. Waterman and Vanita M. Gibbs. Terre Haute: Indiana State University, School of Education, Curriculum Research and Development Center, 1980.

1978

Hamm, Russell L., and Maggie Carey. *Minority Ethnic Education in Indiana Public Schools: A Status Study.* Terre Haute, Ind.: Curriculum Research and Development Center, 1978.

Hamm, Russell L. and Maggie Carey. "Dysfunction in School Administration." *NASSP Bulletin* 62 (February 1978).

Snyder, Joyce, and Russell L. Hamm. *Black People in America: A Teaching-Learning Unit.* Terre Haute, Ind.: Curriculum Research and Development Center, 1978.

1977

Cox, Bertha, and Russell L. Hamm. *101 Old Recipes.* Privately printed.

Findley, Dale, and Russell L. Hamm. "The Bandwagon Approach to Curricular Innovation: Look Before You Leap." *NASSP Bulletin* 61 (October 1977).

Hamm, Russell L. "Swing Back to Basics." C/C + Midwest Program for Minorities in Engineering, Purdue University, West Lafayette, mimeo.

———. Introduction. *Curricular Trends in Indiana Public Schools,* by Fred Snyder, William Clary, and Joseph Ridgely. Terre

Haute, Ind.: Curriculum Research and Development Center, 1977.

Hamm, Russell L., and William E. Brownson. *The Arenas of Power: Focus on Schooling.* Terre Haute: Curriculum Research and Development Center, Indiana State University, 1977.

Sa'ad, Farouk, and Russell L. Hamm. "Teacher Autonomy and/or Administrative Leadership." *Contemporary Education* 48, no. 4 (Summer, 1977).

1976

Hamm, Russell L. "A – is for the Advantages of a Self-Contained Classroom." *Minnesota Elementary Principal* (Silver Anniversary Issue, 1951–76), 19, no. 2 (Winter, 1976).

———. "The Answers Are Easy, the Questions Are Hard." *Junior High-Middle School Bulletin* 14, no. 3 (Spring 1976).

———. "Secondary High School Program." In *A Curriculum Study for the Avon Community School Corporation,* ed. Leland D. Melvin. Avon: Indiana State University, School of Education, 1976.

Hamm, Russell L. and Michael P. Benway. "A Bicentennial Essay: Progress . . . or Paradox." *Junior High-Middle School Bulletin* 14, no. 2 (Winter 1976).

Hamm, Russell L. and Thomas Knarr. "Ferment and Foreshadowing—1976–1830." *Contemporary Education* 47, no. 3 (Spring 1976).

Morris, Robert C., and Russell L. Hamm. "Toward a Curriculum Theory." *Educational Leadership* 33, no. 4 (January 1976).

Van Til, William, William E. Brownson, and Russell L. Hamm. "Back to Basics—with a Difference." *Education Digest* 41, no. 5 (January 1976).

1975

Hamm, Russell L. "The Educational Program." In *A Cooperative Study of the South-West Parke County Community School Corpo-*

ration, edited by Leland D. Melvin. Terre Haute: Indiana State University, School of Education, 1975.

————. "The Educational Program." In *A Cooperative Study of the Hobart Township Community School Corporation,* edited by Leland D. Melvin. Terre Haute: Indiana State University, School of Education, 1975.

Hamm, Russell L. and Dale G. Findley. "On Being Human: Guidelines for Teachers." *Contemporary Education* 46, no. 4 (Summer 1975).

Hamm, Russell L. and Richard D. Spear. *Environmental Education in Indiana Public Schools.* Terre Haute: Curriculum Research and Development Center, Indiana State University, School of Education, 1975.

Van Til, William, William E. Brownson, and Russell L. Hamm. "Back to Basics—with a Difference." *Educational Leadership* 33, no. 1 (October 1975).

1974

Bough, Max E. and Russell L. Hamm. *The American Intermediate School.* Danville, Ill.: Interstate Printers and Publishers, 1974.

Fakouri, M. E., and Russell L. Hamm. "Achievement Motivation, Dogmatism, and Philosophical Orientation." *Psychology: A Journal of Human Behavior* 2, no. 1 (February 1974).

Hamm, Russell L. *Philosophy and Education: Alternatives in Theory and Practice.* Danville, Ill.: Interstate Printers and Publishers, 1974.

————. "What Do You Mean, Open Education." *Contemporary Education* 44, no. 3 (Spring 1974).

————. Three poems. *Twigs* X/2 (Spring 1974).

————. "The Myth of Objectivity." *Clearing House* 48 (May 1974).

Morris, Robert E. and Russell L. Hamm. "Alternative Instructional Theories." *New Voices in Education* 3, no. 4 (Spring 1974).

1972

Hamm, Russell L., "Hoosier Educators: Charles A. Beard." *Contemporary Education* 43 (February 1972).

————. "Existential Poetry." *Contemporary Education* 44, no. 2 (November 1972).

Hamm, Russell L. and Vicki Arnolt. "The Existential View of Affective Learning." *Contemporary Education* 44, no. 2 (November 1972).

1971

Hamm, Russell L., *Hooks for the Darkness*. San Antonio, Tex.: Naylor Company, 1971.

————. *Intraclass Grouping in the Secondary School*. Danville, Ill.: Interstate Printers and Publishers, Inc., 1971.

————. "Philosophical Reflections on the Drug Crises in Schools." In *Critical Health Issues Workshop*. Terre Haute, Ind.: Department of Health and Safety, Indiana State University, 1971.

————. "Hoosier Educators: Henry Lester Smith." *Contemporary Education* 43 (October 1971).

————. "Are Curriculum Guides Passé?" *The Clearing House* 46, no. 4 (December 1971).

Hamm, Russell L. and Max E. Bough, eds. *Yearbook of Indiana Education*. Danville, Ill.: Interstate Printers and Publishers, 1971.

Walker, William E., and Russell L. Hamm. *Innovations in Indiana Schools*. Terre Haute, Ind.: Curriculum Research and Development Center, School of Education, 1971.

1970

Hamm, Russell. *Under the Hamm Ham Tree: Hypothesis and History*. Danville, Ill., privately printed, 1970.

————. "Intra-Class Grouping in Social Studies in the Intermediate Grades." In *Social Studies Education for Young Americans*, by Ralph H. Jones Kendall. Dubuque, Iowa: Hunt Publishing Company, 1970.

————. "Middle School vs. Junior High School." *Clearing House* 44, no. 5 (January 1970).

————. "Intraclass Grouping in Literature." *Indiana English Journal* 4, no. 1–2 (Winter 1970).

―――. "What is IASCD?," *The Hoosier Schoolmaster of the Seventies* 9, no. 3 (February 1970).

Hamm, Russell L., and Max E. Bough, (eds.), *Yearbook of Indiana Education*. Danville, Ill.: Interstate Printers and Publishers, Inc., 1970.

Hamm, Russell L. and David Kelsey. "The Evolution of Supervision." *Indiana ASCD News*, April 1970.

Hamm, Russell L. and William L. Walker. *Content, Media, and Special Services Supervisors*. Terre Haute, Ind.: Curriculum Research and Development Center, School of Education, Indiana State University, March 1970.

Hamm, Russell L. and William L. Walker. "Preparation of Curriculum Workers. *Educational Leadership* 28, no. 1 (October 1970).

Walker, William L. and Russell L. Hamm. "Role and Status of Indiana Curriculum Workers." *Contemporary Education* 41, no. 6 (May 1970).

1969

Russell L. Hamm. "The Evolving Elementary School Curriculum." In *Educational Perspectives of the Elementary School* by Ralph H. Jones and Benjamin Walker. Dubuque, Iowa: W. M. C. Brown Book Company, 1969.

―――. "Paradox and Promise." WVSEC *Spotlight* (February 1969).

―――. "Conservation Education—Yes!" *The Hoosier Schoolmaster of the Sixties* 8, no. 6 (April 1969).

―――. "A is for the Advantages of a Self-Contained Classroom." *Minnesota Elementary School Principal* 10, no. 6 (May 1969).

Hamm, Russell L. and William L. Walker. *Role and Status of Curriculum Workers in Indiana*. Terre Haute, Ind.: Curriculum Research and Development Center, School of Education, Indiana State University, 1969.

1968

Hamm, Russell L. "The Educational Program." In *A Cooperative Study of the Northeast Sullivan School Corporation*, edited by John Hill. Terre Haute, Indiana: Curriculum Research and Development Center, Indiana State University, 1968.

———. "Why American Studies?" *Civic Leader* 46, no. 21 (February 26, 1968).

———. "Selected for Review—Learning by Discovery, Explorations in Creativity, and Behavioral Science Frontiers in Education." *Educational Leadership* 25, no. 8 (May 1968).

Hamm, Russell L. and Victoria Jacobson. "Intraclass Grouping in Reading." *Reading Improvement* 5, no. 2 (Fall 1968).

Hamm, Russell L. and Mrs. Marjorie Jerry. "Individualizing Instruction in Home Economics through Intraclass Grouping." *Indiana ASCD News* 9, no. 5 (June 1968).

1967

Hamm, Russell L. *Conservation Education in Indiana Schools.* Terre Haute, Ind.: Curriculum Research and Development Center, School of Education, Indiana State University, 1967.

———. "Process and Procedure." In *Family Finance Education: An Interdisciplinary Approach*, vol. 1, edited by Mary Gibbs, Byron Brown, and Harriet Darrow. Terre Haute, Ind.: Center for Education in Family Finance, Indiana State University, 1967.

———. Review of *Process and Content: Curriculum Design and the Application of Knowledge*, by J. Cecil Parker and Louis L. Rubin, *Indiana ASCD News*, January 1967.

———. "Core Curriculum at the Crossroads." *Teachers College Journal* 39, no. 2 (November 1967).

———. Review of *Teaching in a World of Changes*, by Robert H. Anderson, in *Teacher's College Journal* 39 (October 1967).

1966

Hamm, Russell L., *A Study of the Physical Facilities, Personnel, Curriculum and Instruction of Paris High School.* Paris, Ill.: Paris Union School District No. 95, Division of Extended Services, School Survey Services, 1966.

———. "Structures and/or Structure." *Curriculum Leadership* 3, no. 3 (May 1966).

———. "Junior High School: The Uniquely American Institution." *Junior High School Newsletter,* Fall 1966.

Rentschler, James, and Russell L. Hamm. *A Curriculum Study of the South Knox School Corporation,* Bureau of School Administrative Services, School of Education, 1966.

1965

Hamm, Russell L. "A Current Events Rationale." *Social Studies* 56, no. 1 (January 1965).

———. "A New Awakening in Conservation Education." *Minnesota Journal of Education* 46, no. 3 (November 1965).

1964

Hamm, Russell L. *A Teaching Learning Unit on Civil Rights.* St. Paul, Minn.: Roseville Schools, 1964.

Hamm, Russell L. ed. *Research Studies: Roseville School District. A Study of Ramsey Dropouts in the Classes of 1958, 1959, 1960, and 1961. A Study of Industrial Arts in the Roseville School District. A Study of Home Economics in the Roseville School District. A Study of Newspaper Approach to Teaching Current Events in the Roseville Schools.* St. Paul, Minn.: Roseville Schools, 1964.

Hamm, Russell L. and Larry Nason. *An Ecological Approach to Conservation.* Minneapolis, Minn.: Burgess Publishing Company, 1964.

Jarvi, Marjorie and Russell L. Hamm. "The Other Side of the

Paperback Question." *Curriculum Leadership* 1, no. 2 (May 1964).

Jensen, Kenneth M. and Russell L. Hamm. *Classroom Control.* Roseville Schools, 1964.

1963

Hamm, Russell L. *As Sounding Brass.* New York: Vantage Press, 1963.

———. "Methods of Teaching and Learning in the Junior High School." *NASSP Bulletin,* October 1963.

———. "Establish A Research Council." *Clearing House* 38, no. 4 (December 1963).

———. "An Integrated Program for the Gifted." *Minnesota Journal of Education* 44, no. 5 (December 1963), p. 8.

Jacobson, Victoria and Russell L. Hamm. "Should We Have Language Instruction in the Elementary Schools?" *The Minnesota Elementary Principal* 5, no. 1 (Fall 1963).

1962

Hamm, Russell L., *Supplementary Units for Applied Biology.* St. Paul, Minn.: Roseville Schools, 1962.

———. "The Foreign Language Club: Ideal for the Junior High." *School Activities* 33, no. 8 (April 1962).

———. "New Approaches to Articulation." *Bulletin of the Minnesota Association of Secondary School Principals* 26, no. 2 (November 1962).

Hamm, Russell L. and Gene K. Hanson. *Minnesota: A Teaching Guide.* Minneapolis, Minn., Burgess Publishing Company, 1962.

1961

Hamm, Russell L. *Christmas Card.* Printed privately, 1961.

———. "The Junior High School Differs." *Clearing House* 35, no. 8, (April 1961).

————. "The Life of Nellie Belles MacMillan." *Owen Leader* 48, no. 32, (July 1961).

————. "Background of the Core Curriculum." *Kor* 1, no. 1, (December 1960).

1960

Hamm, Russell L. *Core Curriculum As Conceived By Junior High School Teachers of Core and by Junior High School Principals of Schools that Have Core Programs in the State of Minnesota.* Thesis, Indiana University, 1960.

1958

Hamm, Russell L. *On the Bridge.* St. Cloud, Minn.: Sentinel Press, 1958.

————. "Criticism and the Social Studies." *Social Education* 22, no. 7 (November 1958).

1957

Hamm, Russell L. "Youth Serve Their Community." *School Activities* 29, no. 1 (September 1957).

1956

Hamm, Russell L., "J. J. Jones and Defeat." In *Epos Anthology.* Lake Como, Fla.: New Athenaeum Press, 1956.

————. "One." *Calamus,* 1956.

————. "Arlington at Midnight." *Cornucopia* 9, (January 1956).

————. "My Bluebird," "Summer," and "The Cardinal." *Cornucopia* 9, (March 1956).

————. "From Clark's Bridge." *The Step Ladder* 39, no. 4 (Spring 1956).

———. "The Philosopher" and "Thoughts." *Starlanes: The International Quarterly of Science Fiction Poetry*, April 1956.
———. "Philosophy." *Caravan: Hawkeye Poetry Magazine* 1, no. 6 (September–October) 1956.

1955

Hamm, Russell L. "Grouseland." In *This Shall Endure: Avalon Anthology*. Alpine, Tex.: Different Press, 1955.
———. "Rural Scene." *Appalachian News Express* (1955).
———. "Squirrel Hunter." *American Weave, Twentieth Quarterly* 20, no. 1 (1955).
———. "Ab Orr Usque Ad Mala." *American Courier* 16, no. 1 (January 1, 1955).
———. "Conflict." *American Courier* 16, no. 2 (February 1, 1955), p. 23.
———. "Awakening." *American Courier* 16, no. 3 (March 1, 1955).
———. "Lilacs I Love." *Midland Poetry Review* 24, no. 87 (Spring 1955).
———. "Spring." *Cornucopia* 8 (April 1955).
———. "To Mary Edith." *American Courier* 16, no. 3 (April 1, 1955).
———. "In Spring," *American Courier* 16, no. 5 (May 1, 1955).
———. "Five Fathoms Five in Fescally." *American Courier* 16, no. 6 (June 1, 1955).
———. "Earthbound." *Midland Poetry Review* 24, no. 88 (Summer 1955).
———. "Grandmother." *American Courier* 16, no. 7 (July 1, 1955).
———. "Dali's Crucifixion." *Flame* 11, no. 3 (Autumn 1955).
———. "Window of the Soul." *Candor: A Magazine for Writers and Thinkers* 17, no. 2 (October 1955).
———. "Pigeon Music," *Section Eight*, December, 1955.
Hamm, Russell, L., and Mrs. Blanchealine Johnson. "Democracy (play)." *The Indiana Social Studies Quarterly*, Spring 1955.

1954

Hamm, Russell L. "Hope." *New Atheneum*, Winter 1954.
———. "Operation Glory." *Midland Poetry Review* 23, no. 86 (Winter 1954).
———. "Prison." *Epos*, Winter 1954.
———. "Sarah Lincoln." *Cornucopia* 7 (February 1954).
———. "Death in Headlines." *Cornucopia* 7, no. 8 (May 1954).
———. "Night Sky." *Cornucopia* 8, (November 8, 1954).
———. "Conscience." *American Courier* 15, no. 12 (December 1, 1954).

1953

Hamm, Russell L. "Parted" and "The Lost Dove." *Cornucopia*, no. 4, (January 1953).
———. "The Ruby Throat." *The Chaparral Writer*.
———. "Friendship," "Knowing,""Essence," "Of Love," "Living," "Ambition." *Indianapolis News: Hoosier Homespun*, 1953.

1950–52

Hamm, Russell L., *Genamica*. Gosport, Ind.: C. A. Wampler Publishing Company, 1950.
———. "Requiem," and "The Conception of Owen County." *Owen Leader*, 1950–52.
———. "One More Spring," "Salesmanship," "Prayer," "The Coming of Night," "Carving," "This Hope," "To Poets," "Dead Souls," "Silence," "Obsequious," "Premonition," "Realism," "Remember," "Bethshan," and "March." *Indianapolis News: Hoosier Homespun*, 1950–52.

1944–45

Hamm, Russell L., "Quincy School News." *Owen Leader*, 1944–45.